AA

walking in the
Cotswolds

Discover idyllic stone

villages, tranquil valleys

and rolling countryside.

First published 2006

Produced by AA Publishing
© Automobile Association Developments Limited 2006

Published by AA Publishing (a trading name of Automobile Association Developments Limited, whose registered office is Fanum House, Basing View, Basingstoke, Hampshire RG21 4EA; registered number 1878835)

Ordnance Survey® This product includes mapping data licensed from Ordnance Survey® with the permission of the Controller of Her Majesty's Stationery Office.
© Crown copyright 2006. All rights reserved. Licence number 399221

ISBN-10: 0-7495-4847-9
ISBN-13: 978-0-7495-4847-6

A02781

A CIP catalogue record for this book is available from the British Library.

The contents of this book are believed correct at the time of printing. Nevertheless, the publishers cannot be held responsible for any errors or omissions or for changes in the details given in this book or for the consequences of any reliance on the information it provides. This does not affect your statutory rights. We have tried to ensure accuracy in this book, but things do change and we would be grateful if readers would advise us of any inaccuracies they may encounter.

We have taken all reasonable steps to ensure that these walks are safe and achievable by walkers with a realistic level of fitness. However, all outdoor activities involve a degree of risk and the publishers accept no responsibility for any injuries caused to readers whilst following these walks. For more advice on walking safely see page 112.

Some of these routes may appear in other AA walks books.

Visit the AA Publishing website at www.theAA.com/bookshop

Layouts by Liz Baldin at Bookwork Creative Associates Ltd, Hampshire, for AA Publishing

Printed by Leo Paper Group in China

PREVIOUS PAGE: The Cotswold Way
RIGHT: Views from Painswick Beacon
PAGE 6: Cranham Woods

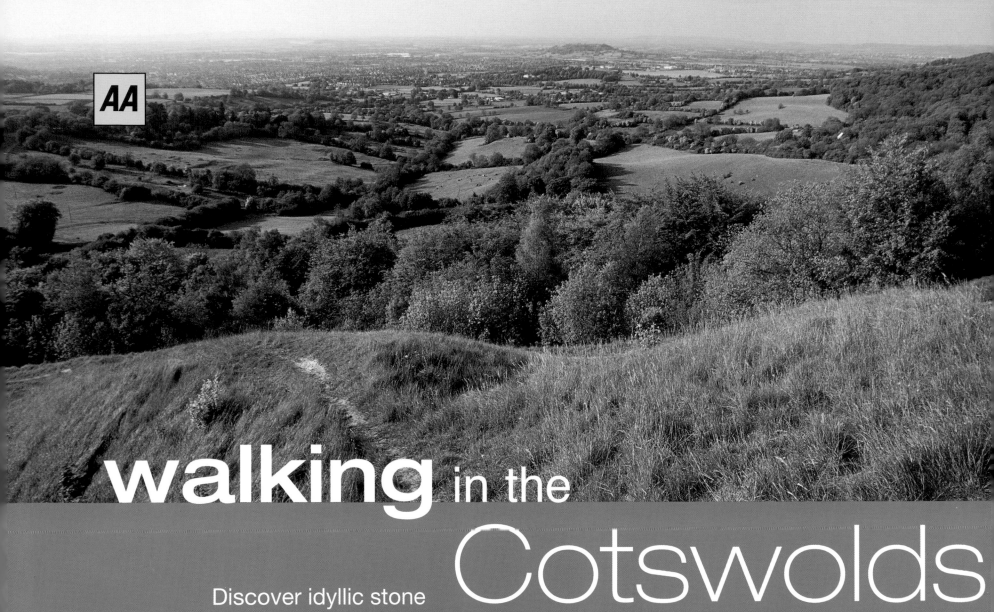

walking in the Cotswolds

Discover idyllic stone villages, tranquil valleys and rolling countryside.

Contents

This superb selection of walks introduces the themes and characters that define the beautiful landscape of the Cotswolds.

Introducing the Cotswolds

For many people, the Cotswolds epitomise a vision of rural England. Here are pretty golden-stone villages, huddled in tranquil wooded valleys, bisected by sparkling brooks and surrounded by evergreen farmland. But for many too, this vision is unrealised. The crowds that throng around Broadway and Bourton-on-the-Water, buying their ice creams and enjoying the various tourist 'attractions' are surely missing something. Take a bit more time to explore this region and you will see that sometimes the myth and the reality can be reconciled, especially if you are prepared to step out of your car and get your boots muddy.

Protected

The whole region is protected by the Cotswolds Area of Outstanding Natural Beauty (AONB), at 790 square miles (2038 sq km) it is the largest area in the country to be designated in this way. In the east, these 'official' Cotswolds reach surprisingly deep into Oxfordshire, to the north they point green fingers into both Warwickshire and Worcestershire, in the south, Wiltshire and North East Somerset claim their portions, but the lion's share of this beautiful landscape falls in Gloucestershire, and you will find this is where the majority of the walks in this guide are too.

Changing Scenery

Approaching the Cotswolds from the north east, you'll notice the scenery begins to change in subtle ways. The half-timber and thatch of 'Shakespeare Country' begins to give way to a honey-coloured stone that defines the borders of the region. This is the oolitic limestone that tilts down from west to east. In the east, the gradually rising profile is virtually indistinguishable. One is only vaguely aware that the surrounding countryside is gaining in altitude. This is open, arable farming country, punctuated by dark stands of trees and rivers flanked by water-meadows. Here you will find the source of the mighty Thames.

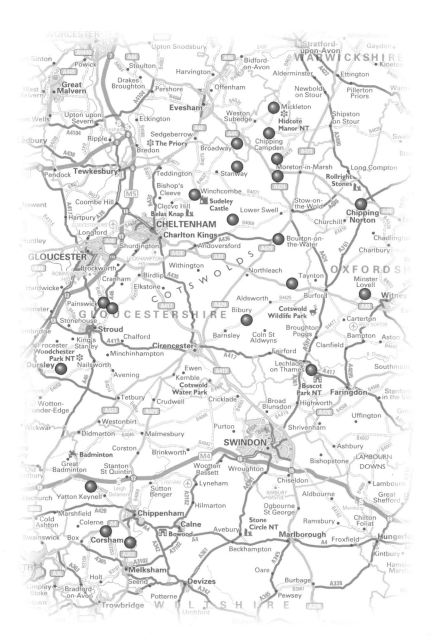

Although the watershed is hardly apparent, the presence of two great east-west canals hints that it may have once presented a formidable obstacle to transport. These waterways – the Thames and Severn and the Kennet and Avon canals – provide some of the best level walking in the southern Cotswolds and cut through the very heart of the suddenly dramatic valleys that emerge on the western side.

Idyllic

However, it is the idyllic stone-built villages that attract visitors to all parts of the Cotswolds, and on these walks you will find out why. In Snowshill, Bibury, Castle Combe and Stanton, the impossibly lovely buildings will take your breath away. And in Chipping Campden, you'll feel you have found the epicentre of this vernacular wealth. The townscapes are sublime too, as you'll find at Corsham and Burford. There is an intimacy about these warm buildings that never fails to thrill and inspire locals and visitors alike. You will not be the first to experience the uplifting charm of the Cotswolds. Thousands of years ago ancient peoples were moved to commemorate the burial of their dead on these undulating hills. At Belas Knap, you'll find one of the best preserved remnants of such burials, and at the Rollright Stones you may wonder at what insights these early folk possessed when they lined up their megalithic arrays with the midsummer moon.

Fine Buildings

Vernacular architecture in the Cotswolds undoubtedly provides many of the stars of the built environment, but there are some grand houses too. There's nothing here on the scale of Longleat or Blenheim, but you'll find Sezincote and Compton Wynyates delightful nevertheless. Church buildings are also an impressive part of this legacy. The romantic remains of Hailes Abbey sit quietly at the foot of the escarpment and are best seen from the footpath near Beckbury Camp, where Thomas Cromwell surveyed their destruction for Henry VIII. Among the outstanding churches, Chipping Camden is a tribute to the wealth of the medieval wool trade and the twin churches at Eastleach Turville and Eastleach Martin eye each other across the River Leach.

using this book

Information Panels
An information panel for each walk shows its relative difficulty, the distance and total amount of ascent (that is how much ascent you will accumulate throughout the walk). An indication of the gradients you will encounter is shown by the rating ▲▲▲ (fairly flat ground with no steep slopes) to ▲▲▲ (undulating terrain with several very steep slopes).

Minimum Time
The minimum time suggested is for approximate guidance only. It assumes reasonably fit walkers and doesn't allow for stops.

Suggested Maps
Each walk has a suggested map. This will usually be a 1:25,000 scale Ordnance Survey Explorer map.

Start Points
The start of each walk is given as a six-figure grid reference, prefixed by two letters indicating which 100km square of the National Grid it refers to. You'll find more information on grid references on most Ordnance Survey maps.

Dogs
We have tried to give dog owners useful advice about how dog friendly each walk is. Please respect other countryside users. Keep your dog under control at all times, especially around livestock, and obey local bylaws and other dog control notices. Remember it is against the law to let your dog foul in many public areas, especially in villages and towns.

Car Parking
Many of the car parks suggested are public, but occasionally you may find you have to park on the roadside or in a lay-by. Please be considerate when you leave your car, ensuring that access roads or gates are not blocked and that other vehicles can pass safely. Remember that pub car parks are private and should not be used unless you have the owner's permission.

Maps
Each walk is accompanied by a sketch map drawn from the Ordnance Survey map and appended with the author's local observations. The scale of these maps varies from walk to walk. Some routes have a suggested option in the same area with a brief outline of the possible route. You will need a current Ordnance Survey map to make the most of these suggestions.

Hill Country

Buildings and villages are not for everyone though and, at its western edge, the Cotswold escarpment can hold its own for lovers of wide views. From Dover's Hill down to Uley Bury, you'll see faraway Wales, the Forest of Dean and the Malvern Hills, as well as catching some fine panoramas of the Cotswolds themselves rising up from the Severn Plain and Vale of Evesham. The Cotswold Way National Trail follows this edge for much of its 101-mile (163-km) route.

Historic Landscape

This is the land where Laurie Lee grew up, made famous by his evocative childhood memories in Cider with Rosie. Here Arts and Crafts pioneers rediscovered pre-industrial values in design and created everything from glassware to revolutionary gardens. A century before, the Industrial Revolution transformed the local woollen industry, bringing great mills to the Stroud Valley and poverty to the old weaving villages. Much of the Cotswolds' history is tied to the fortunes of wool. At one time this was the wool capital of Europe. The elaborate medieval churches are testimonies to the wealth of their merchant patrons, but you'll find precious few sheep on the hills now. Agricultural changes over the last century almost brought the local 'Cotswold Lion' breed to extinction. Now your only glimpse of these fine beasts might be in one of the rare breeds centres. Whilst the stone walls and tight fields of pastoral farming survive on the poorer soils, arable dominates the Cotswold landscape.

Off the Beaten Path

Walk through this ever-changing landscape and see how little has actually changed over the centuries. The woods, the villages, the hidden valleys and surprising elevations remain. This apparent contradiction reflects the region's historical ability to reinvent itself and is why new generations of visitors will always discover the region for themselves. This selection of 20 walks introduces the themes and characters that created this living, beautiful landscape.

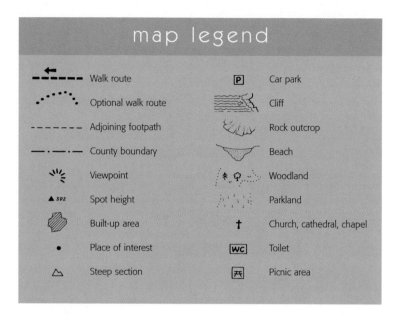

map legend			
← ▪▪▪▪▪▪	Walk route	P	Car park
▪▪▪▪▪▪	Optional walk route		Cliff
▪ ▪ ▪ ▪ ▪ ▪ ▪	Adjoining footpath		Rock outcrop
▪ — ▪ — ▪ —	County boundary		Beach
	Viewpoint		Woodland
▲ 392	Spot height		Parkland
	Built-up area	†	Church, cathedral, chapel
•	Place of interest	WC	Toilet
△	Steep section	🔳	Picnic area

ABOVE: Longrynd, Church Stretton
RIGHT: Fields near Broughton Castle

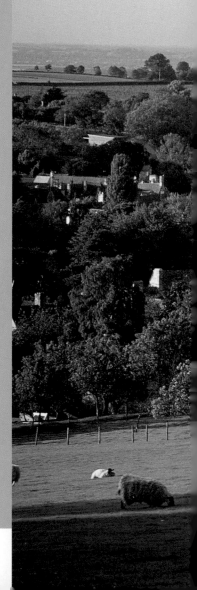

*Walk out from the Cotswolds' most beautiful
wool town to Dover's Hill, the spectacular site
of centuries-old Whitsuntide festivities.*

Olimpick Playground near Chipping Campden

The Cotswold Olimpicks bear only a passing resemblance to their more famous international counterpart. What they lack in grandeur and razzmatazz, however, they make up for in picturesque prettiness and local passion. Far from being one of the multi-million dollar shrines to technology which seem so vital to the modern Olympics, the stadium is a natural amphitheatre – the summit of Dover's Hill, on the edge of the Cotswold escarpment. The hill, with spectacular views westwards over the Vale of Evesham, is an English version of the site of the Greek original.

ABOVE: *Dry-stone wall, Sheep Street*
RIGHT: *Overlooking Chipping Campden*

Royal Assent

Dover's Hill is named after the founder of the Cotswold Olimpicks, Robert Dover. Established with the permission of James I, they were dubbed 'royal' games, and indeed have taken place during the reign of fourteen monarchs. Dover was born in Norfolk in 1582. He was educated at Cambridge and then was called to the bar. His profession brought him to the Cotswolds but he had vivid memories of the plays and spectacles that he had seen in the capital, for this was the era of William Shakespeare.

It is generally accepted that the first games took place in 1612, but they may well have begun at an earlier date. It is also possible that Dover was simply reviving an existing ancient festivity. Initially, at least, the main events were horse-racing and hare-coursing, the prizes being, respectively, a silver castle ornament and a silver-studded collar. Other competitions in these early games were for running, jumping, throwing, wrestling and staff fighting. The area was festooned with yellow flags and ribbons and there were many dancing events, as well as pavilions for chess and other similarly cerebral contests.

Annual Event

The Olimpicks soon became an indispensable part of the local Whitsuntide festivities, with mention of them even being made in Shakespeare's work. Robert Dover managed the games for 30 years and he died in 1652. The games continued in a variety of forms throughout the following centuries, surviving several attempts to suppress them when they became more rowdy and seemed to present a threat to public order and safety. They finally became an established annual event once again in 1966.

LEFT: Sheep Street, Chipping Campden

Nowadays, the games are a more like a cross between pantomime and carnival, but they have somehow retained their atmosphere of local showmanship. At the end of the evening's events all the spectators, holding flaming torches, file down the road back into Chipping Campden, where the festivities continue with dancing and music along the main street and in the square.

It's worth lingering in Chipping Campden, before or after the walk. Possibly the most beautiful of all the Cotswold towns, it was once famous throughout Europe as the centre of the English wool trade. A leisurely stroll along its curving High Street of handsome stone houses should be an essential part of your visit. The church is particularly fine and it's also worthwhile searching out the Ernest Wilson Memorial Garden, on the High Street.

BELOW: Perpendicular tower of St James, Chipping Campden

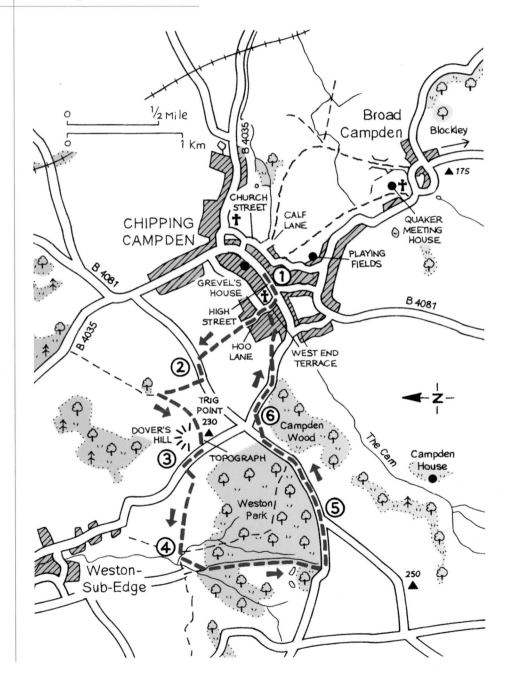

walk information

➤ **DISTANCE**	5 miles (8km)
➤ **MINIMUM TIME**	2hrs
➤ **ASCENT/GRADIENT**	280ft (85m) ▲▲▲
➤ **LEVEL OF DIFFICULTY**	🏃🏃🏃
➤ **PATHS**	Fields, roads and tracks, 8 stiles
➤ **LANDSCAPE**	Open hillside, woodland and village
➤ **SUGGESTED MAP**	OS Explorer OL45 The Cotswolds
➤ **START/FINISH**	Grid reference: SP 151391
➤ **DOG FRIENDLINESS**	Suitable in parts (particularly Dover's Hill) but livestock in some fields
➤ **PARKING**	Chipping Campden High Street or in the main square
➤ **PUBLIC TOILETS**	A short way down Sheep Street
➤ **CONTRIBUTOR**	Christopher Knowles

walk directions

1 Turn left from the **Noel Arms**, continue to the **Catholic church**, and turn right into **West End Terrace**. Where this bears right, go straight ahead on **Hoo Lane**. Follow this up to a right turn, with farm buildings on your left. Continue uphill over a stile to a path and keep going to a road.

2 Turn left for a few paces and then right to cross to a path. Follow this along the field edge to a stile. Go over to **Dover's Hill** and follow the hedge to a stile with extensive views before you. Turn left along the escarpment edge, which drops away to your right. Pass a **trig point** and then a **topograph**. Now go right, down the slope, to a kissing gate on the left. Go through to a road and turn right.

3 After 150yds (137m) turn left over a stile into a field. Cross this and find a gate in the bottom right-hand corner. Head

straight down the next field. At a stile go into another field and, keeping to the left of a fence, continue to another stile. Head down the next field, cross a track and then find adjacent stiles in the bottom left corner.

4 Cross the first one and walk along the bottom of a field. Keep the stream and fence to your right and look for a stile in the far corner. Go over, crossing the stream, and then turn left, following a rising woodland path alongside the stream. Enter a field through a gate and continue ahead to meet a track. Stay on this, passing through gateposts, until you come to a country lane and turn left.

5 After 400yds (366m) reach a busier road and turn left for a further 450yds (411m). Shortly before the road curves left, drop to the right on to a field path parallel with the road. About 200yds (183m) before the next corner go half right down the field to a road.

6 Turn right, down the road. Shortly after a cottage on the right, go left into a field. Turn right to cross over a stile and go half left to the corner. Pass through a kissing gate, cross a road among houses and continue ahead to meet **West End Terrace**. Turn right to return to the centre of **Chipping Campden**.

LEFT: *Main Street, Chipping Campden*

17

A rewarding walk above a thriving Cotswold village and the burial place of Henry's sixth queen – Catherine Parr.

Winchcombe and Sudeley Castle

The first castle was built here in 1140. Originally little more than a fortified manor house, by the mid-15th century Sudeley had acquired a keep and courtyards. It became a royal castle after the Wars of the Roses before being given to Thomas Seymour, Edward VI's Lord High Admiral. Seymour lived at Sudeley with his wife, Catherine Parr. He was executed for treason and the castle passed to Catherine's brother, William, but he was also executed. Queen Mary gave the property to Sir John Brydges, the first Lord Chandos. A Royalist stronghold during the Civil War, it was disarmed by the Parliamentarians and left to decay until its purchase by the Dent brothers in 1863.

ABOVE: *Gargoyle decoration on St Peter's Church, Winchcombe*
RIGHT: *Sudeley Castle, Winchcombe*

walk information

➤ **DISTANCE**	4 miles (6.4km)
➤ **MINIMUM TIME**	2hrs
➤ **ASCENT/GRADIENT**	490ft (150m) ▲▲▲
➤ **LEVEL OF DIFFICULTY**	🚶🚶🚶
➤ **PATHS**	Fields and lanes, 10 stiles
➤ **LANDSCAPE**	Woodland, hills and villages
➤ **SUGGESTED MAP**	OS Explorer OL45 The Cotswolds
➤ **START/FINISH**	Grid reference: SP 024282
➤ **DOG FRIENDLINESS**	On leads (or close control) throughout – much livestock
➤ **PARKING**	Free on Abbey Terrace; also car park on Back Lane
➤ **PUBLIC TOILETS**	On corner of Vine Street
➤ **CONTRIBUTOR**	Christopher Knowles

5 Just before the house turn right, cross the field and go over a stile. In the next field go to the bottom left-hand corner to emerge on a road. Turn left and, after a few paces, turn right along a lane, towards **Sudeley Lodge Parks Farm**.

6 Opposite a cottage turn right on to a footpath across a field. At the bottom nip over a stile and turn right. At the next corner turn left, remaining in the same field. Cross another stile, continue for a few paces and then turn right over a stile. Walk half left, following the obvious waymarkers to a fence, with **Sudeley Castle** now on your right-hand side.

7 Go through two kissing gates to enter the park area. Cross a drive and then cross a field to another gate. Go through this and bear half right to the farthest corner. You will emerge on **Castle Street** in Winchcombe, where you can turn left to return to the village centre.

LEFT AND ABOVE: The topiary of Sudeley Castle gardens

Through the wooded By Brook

Valley from a famous

picture-book village.

Castle Combe and By Brook

ABOVE: *Dry-stone wall*
LEFT: *The Street passes over By Brook,*
via the Great Town Bridge, Castle Combe

To many, the idyllic village of Castle Combe needs no introduction, since it has featured on countless chocolate-box lids, calendars and jigsaw puzzles. Since being voted 'the prettiest village in England' in 1962, there have been more visitors to it, more photographs taken of it and more words written about it than any other village in the county. Nestling deep in a stream-threaded combe, just a mile (1.6km), and a world away, from the motorway, it certainly has all the elements to make it a tourist's dream.

You'll find 15th-century Cotswold stone cottages with steep gabled roofs surrounding a turreted church and stone-canopied market cross, a medieval manor house, a fast-flowing stream in the main street leading to an ancient packhorse bridge and a perfectly picturesque river. Yet, as preservation is taken so seriously here, a palpable atmosphere of unreality surrounds this tiny 'toytown', where television aerials don't exist, gardens are immaculately kept, and the inevitable commercialism is carefully concealed. Behind this present-day façade, however, exists a fascinating history that's well worth exploring, and the timeless valleys and tumbling wooded hillsides that surround the village are favourite Wiltshire walking destinations. If you don't like crowds and really want to enjoy Castle Combe, undertake this walk on a winter weekday.

'Castlecombe' Cloth

The Castle, which gave the village its name, began life as a Roman fort and was used by the Saxons before becoming a Norman castle in 1135 and the home of the de Dunstanville family. In the 13th and 14th centuries, the village established itself as an important weaving centre as Sir John Fastolf, the lord of the manor, erected fulling mills along the By Brook and provided 50 cottages for his workers. With the growth of the cloth trade in Wiltshire, Castle Combe prospered greatly, becoming more like a town, with a weekly market and an annual fair that was regarded as 'The most celebrated faire in North Wiltshire for sheep.'

The greatest tribute to the great wealth created by the weaving industry is reflected in St Andrew's Church, which was enlarged during the 15th century. Its impressive

LEFT: Weavers' cottages, Castle Combe

Perpendicular tower was built in 1436. For centuries the villages produced a red and white cloth known as Castlecombe. Cloth manufacture began to decline in the early 18th century when the diminutive By Brook was unable to power the larger machinery being introduced. As people moved to the larger towns, Castle Combe became depopulated and returned to an agricultural existence. An annual fair, centred around the Market Cross, continued until 1904, and Castle Combe remained an 'estate' village until 1947, when the whole village was sold at auction.

walk directions

1 Leave the car park via the steps and turn right. At the T-junction, turn right and follow the lane into **Castle Combe**. Keep left at the **Market Cross**, cross the **By Brook** and continue along the road to take the path, signed '**Long Dean**', across the second bridge on your left.

2 Cross a stile and follow the path uphill and then beside the right-hand fence above the valley (**Macmillan Way**). Beyond an open area, gently ascend through woodland to a stile and gate. Cross a further stile and descend into the hamlet of **Long Dean**.

3 Pass the mill and follow the track right to cross the river bridge. At a mill house, keep right and follow the sunken bridleway uphill to a gate. Shortly enter sloping pasture and follow the defined path around the top edge, bearing left to reach a stile and lane.

4 Turn left and descend to the A420 at **Ford**. Turn right along the pavement and shortly turn right again into **Park Lane**. (If you want to visit the White Hart in Ford village, take the road ahead on your left, signed 'Colerne'.) Climb the gravel track and take the footpath left through a squeeze stile.

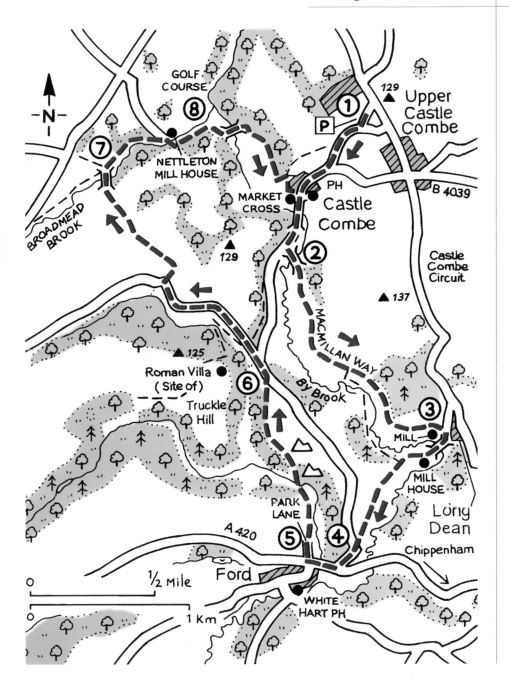

Before mechanisation transformed the wool weaving industry, most weaving took place in the houses of the poor. Firstly, women and children spun the wool either at home or at the workhouse. Then it was transferred to the weavers' houses, who worked on handlooms at piece rates.

A typical weaver's cottage might have had four rooms, with a kitchen and workshop downstairs and a bedroom and storeroom upstairs. There were very few items of furniture in the living rooms, whilst the workroom would have contained a broadloom and some tools. The cloth was then returned to the mill for fulling and cutting. Work on cloth was often a condition of tenure imposed by landlords. The merchant landlord fixed a piecework rate and, provided that the work was satisfactory, the cottage could stay in the weaver's family from generation to generation. Weaving went on this way for some 200 years, until the introduction of steam power in the 18th century. Consequently it tended to take place in the mills of the Stroud Valley. Despite their unfavourable working conditions, the cottage weavers greatly resisted this change but to no avail – the cottage weaving industry went into inexorable decline.

Strictly speaking, much of what is considered picturesque in Bibury is in Arlington, but they are now indistinguishable. Apart from Arlington Row, there is plenty to enjoy in the village, especially the church, which has Saxon origins and is set in pretty gardens. Across the bridge is the old mill, open to the public. Nearby Ablington has an enchanting group of cottages, threaded by the River Coln. A minor classic, *A Cotswold Village* (1898), which describes local life in the late 19th century, was written by J Arthur Gibbs, the squire who lived at Ablington Manor. You pass the walls of the manor on the walk. Close by, further into the village, are a couple of beautiful 18th-century barns.

RIGHT AND FAR RIGHT: Arlington Row in Bibury

walk directions

1 From the parking area opposite the mill, walk along the **Cirencester road**. Immediately after the **Catherine Wheel** pub turn right along a lane and then keep left at a fork. Pass some cottages and go through gates and stiles into a field. Walk on the same line across several stiles and fields until you pass to the right of a house to a road.

2 Turn right and walk down to a junction. Turn right into **Ablington** and cross the bridge. After a few paces, turn left along a track with houses on your right and a stream to your left. Continue to a gate and then follow the track, arriving at another gate after ½ mile (800m).

3 Go into a field and turn sharp right along the valley bottom. Follow a twisting route along the bottom of the valley. When you reach the next gate continue into a field, still following the contours of the valley.

The route will eventually take you through a gate just before a barn and another immediately after.

4 Keep to the track as it bears right and gently ascends a long slope, with woodland to your left. When the track goes sharp right, with a gate before you, turn left through a gate on to a track. Follow it all the way to a road.

5 Turn right. After 250yds (229m), where the road goes right, continue straight on, to enter a track (the **Salt Way**). Continue along this for over ½ mile (800m), until you reach the remains of **Saltway Barn**.

6 Do not walk ahead but, immediately after the barns, turn left into a field and then right along its right-hand margin. Walk on for just under ¾ mile (1.2km), passing hedge and woodland and, where the track breaks to the right, turn right through a gate into a field with a wall on your right.

walk information

➤ **DISTANCE**	6¼ miles (10.1km)
➤ **MINIMUM TIME**	2hrs 30min
➤ **ASCENT/GRADIENT**	165ft (50m) ▲
➤ **LEVEL OF DIFFICULTY**	🚶🚶
➤ **PATHS**	Fields, tracks and lane, may be muddy in places, 6 stiles
➤ **LANDSCAPE**	Exposed wolds, valley, villages and streams
➤ **SUGGESTED MAP**	OS Explorer OL45 The Cotswolds
➤ **START/FINISH**	Grid reference: SP 113068
➤ **DOG FRIENDLINESS**	On leads throughout – there are a lot of sheep and horses
➤ **PARKING**	Bibury village
➤ **PUBLIC TOILETS**	Opposite river on main street, close to Arlington Row
➤ **CONTRIBUTOR**	Christopher Knowles

LEFT: *The River Coln, Bibury*

7 Walk on to pass to the left of **Hale Barn**. Enter a track, with the large buildings of **Bibury Farm** away to your left, and keep on the same line through gates where they arise. Eventually you will descend to a drive which will, in turn, bring you to a road in **Bibury**. Cross the road to walk down between a row of cottages. At the end, near the church and school, turn right. Walk along the pavement into the village, passing **Arlington Row** and the river on your left.

Extending the Walk

You can extend the walk up the **Coln Valley** to **Winson** and **Coln Rogers** by leaving the main route at Point ③ to continue on **Potlickers Lane**. Cross the river and return along the road through the villages until a path brings you back to Point ③ where you can continue the main walk.

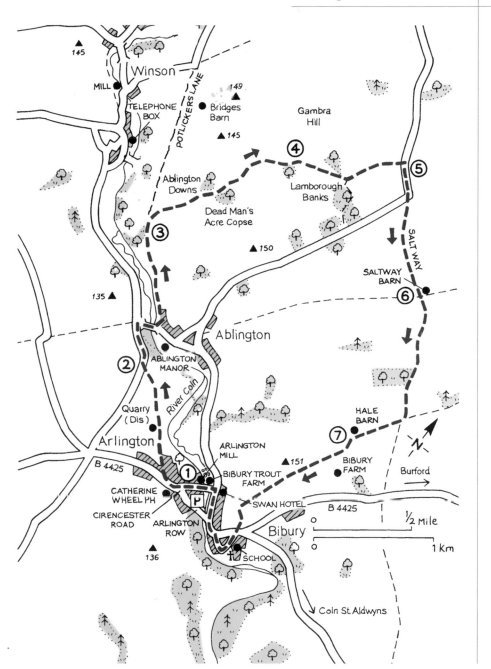

The exotic legacy of a 19th-century diplomat adorns this part of the Cotswold escarpment.

Blockley, Batsford and the Arboretum

ABOVE: *Deer statues in Batsford Arboretum*
LEFT: *High Street in Blockley*

England seems to be a country of trees – it is a feature that visitors often remark on. Walking through Gloucestershire you are surrounded by many native species but when you visit Batsford Arboretum, you will encounter 50 acres (20.3ha) of woodland containing over 1,000 species of trees and shrubs from all over the world, particularly from China, Japan and North America.

The Japanese Connection

The arboretum was originally a garden created in the 1880s by the traveller and diplomat, Bertie Mitford, 1st Lord Redesdale, grandfather to the renowned Mitford sisters. Posted as an attaché to the British Embassy in Tokyo, he became deeply influenced by the Far East. Throughout the park there are bronze statues, brought from Japan by Bertie Mitford, and a wide range of bamboos. After the 1st Lord Dulverton purchased Batsford in 1920, his son transformed the garden into the arboretum we see today, with its 90 species of magnolia, maples, cherry

trees and conifers, all in a beautiful setting on the Cotswold escarpment. Batsford village is comparatively recent, having grown up at the gates of Batsford Park, a neo-Tudor house built between 1888 and 1892 by Ernest George. He built it for Lord Redesdale to replace an earlier, Georgian house. (It is not open to the public but is clearly visible from the arboretum.) Batsford church was constructed a little before the house, in 1862, in a neo-Norman style. It has several monuments to the Mitford family and a fine work by the sculptor Joseph Nollekens from 1808.

Silky Blockley

This walk starts in the unspoilt village of Blockley. It was originally owned by the bishops of Worcester but it didn't really begin to prosper until the 19th century. At one time no fewer than six silk mills, with over 500 employees, were driven by Blockley's fast-flowing stream. Their silks went mostly to Coventry for the production of ribbon. Blockley's history is both enlightened and superstitious. It was one of the first villages in the world to have electric light: in the 1880s Dovedale House was illuminated through Lord Edward Spencer-Churchill's use of water to run a dynamo. In the early part of that same century the millenarian prophetess, Joanna Southcott, lived in the village until her death in 1814. The

walk information

➤ **DISTANCE**	4½ miles (7.2km)
➤ **MINIMUM TIME**	2hrs
➤ **ASCENT/GRADIENT**	410ft (125m) ▲▲
➤ **LEVEL OF DIFFICULTY**	肰
➤ **PATHS**	Lanes, tracks and fields, 8 stiles
➤ **LANDSCAPE**	Woodland, hills with good views and villages
➤ **SUGGESTED MAP**	OS Explorer OL45 The Cotswolds
➤ **START/FINISH**	Grid reference: SP 165348
➤ **DOG FRIENDLINESS**	Some good lengthy stretches without livestock
➤ **PARKING**	On B4479 below Blockley church
➤ **PUBLIC TOILETS**	On edge of churchyard, just off main street in Blockley
➤ **CONTRIBUTOR**	Christopher Knowles

FAR LEFT, LEFT AND BELOW: In the grounds of the superb Batsford Arboretum

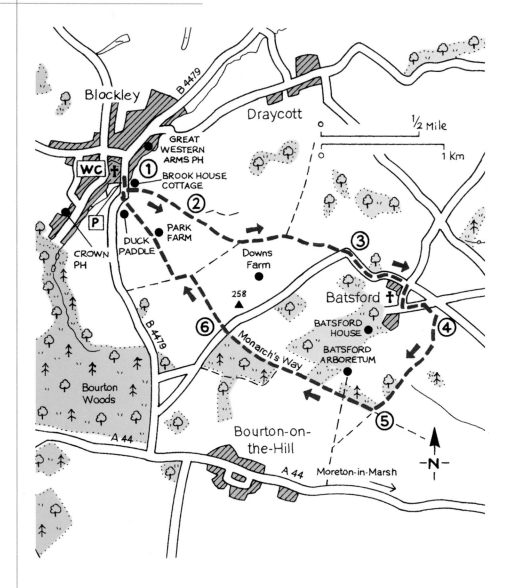

walk directions

1 Walk along the road with the church above you to your right. Continue ahead, pass **Brook House Cottage**, then turn left immediately, up a lane. Follow this as it ascends for ¼ mile (400m) until it bears left.

2 Continue ahead to pass to the right-hand side of a barn. Pass through a gate and in the next field follow its right-hand boundary to another gate. Pass through this to stay on the left side of the next field. Pass into yet another field and then go half right to a gate leading out to a road.

3 Turn left and follow the road down to a crossroads. Turn right to pass through **Batsford** village to a junction (from where you can visit the church on the right). Bear left, and, at the next junction, turn right.

4 After a few paces turn right on to a footpath and follow this through a succession of fields, negotiating stiles and gates where they arise. **Batsford House** will be visible to the right.

5 Finally, go through a gate into a ribbed field and turn right to a stile just left of a house at a drive. Cross this (the entrance to **Batsford Arboretum**), pass through a gate and follow the path up the field to a stile. Cross and continue to a track. Follow this up until where it bears left. Turn right on to a path and almost immediately left at a wall, to continue the ascent. Keep going until you reach a road.

6 Cross the road to go through a gate and pass through two fields until you come to a path among trees. Turn left, go through another gate, and, after a few paces, turn right over a stile into a field with **Blockley** below you. Continue down to a stile at the bottom. Cross into the next field and pass beneath **Park Farm** on your right. Bear gently left, crossing stiles, along the **Duck Paddle**, until you come to a road. Turn right and return to your starting point in the village.

tower of Blockley's substantial church predates the silk boom by only 100 years or so, but inside the church are several imposing monuments to the owners of the local mansion, Northwick Park. At least two of these are by the eminent 18th-century sculptor, John Michael Rysbrack (1694–1770).

A lovely walk through the Windrush Valley to see the disused stone quarries and gain an insight into the character of Cotswold stone.

The Stone Secrets of the Windrush Valley

The Cotswolds, characterised by villages of honey-coloured limestone, lie mainly in Gloucestershire. Stone is everywhere here – walk across any field and shards of oolitic stone lie about the surface like bits of fossilised litter. This limestone, for long an obstacle to arable farming, is a perfect building material. In the past almost every village was served by its own quarry, a few of which are still worked today.

LEFT: St Peter's Church, Windrush

Golden Hue

Limestone is a sedimentary rock, made largely of material derived from living organisms that thrived in the sea that once covered this part of Britain. The rock is therefore easily extracted and easily worked; some of it will actually yield to a handsaw. Of course this is something of a generalisation as, even in a small area, the quality of limestone varies considerably in colour and in texture, suiting certain uses more than others. But it is for its golden hue, due to the presence of iron oxide, that it is most famous.

Slated

The composition of the stone dictates the use to which it will be put. Some limestone, with a high proportion of grit, is best suited to wall building or to hut building. Some outcrops are in very thin layers and are known as 'presents' because they provide almost ready made material for roof-slates. Sometimes the stone needs a little help and in this case it is left out in the winter so that frost freezes the moisture trapped between layers, forcing them apart. The stone can then be shaped into slates and hung on a wooden roof trellis by means of a simple nail. The smallest slates are placed at the top of the roof, the largest at the bottom. Because of their porous nature, they have to overlap and the roof is built at a steep pitch, so that the rain runs off quickly.

Construction Types

There are four basic types of traditional stone construction to be seen in the Cotswolds – dry-stone, mortared rubble, dressed stone and ashlar. Dry-stone, without any mortar, is

LEFT: Houses in Little Barrington

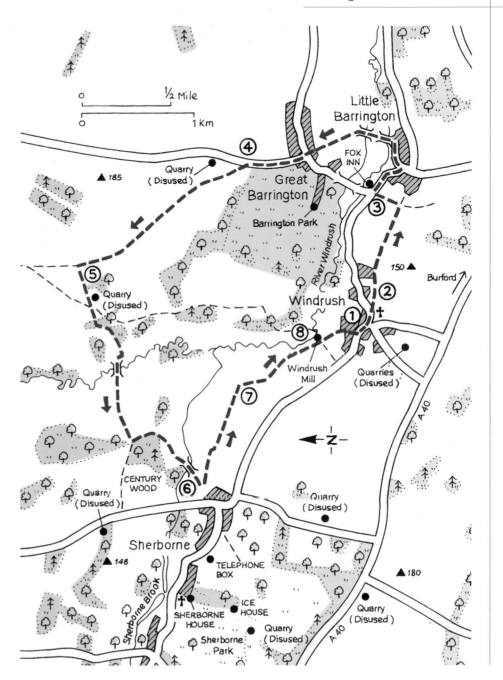

41

used in the many boundary walls you'll see as you walk around the region. Mortared rubble, on the other hand, depends on the use of lime pointing in order to stay upright. You'll see it's use in many of the simpler buildings or as a cheaper backing to buildings faced with better stone. Dressed stone refers to the craft of chopping and axing stone to give it a more polished and tighter finish. This is used in higher order buildings and houses.

Ashlar is the finest technique, where the best stone is sawn and shaped into perfectly aligned blocks that act either as a facing on rubble, or which, more rarely, make up the entire wall. Ashlar was used in the finer houses and, occasionally, in barns. The quality of Cotswold stone has long been recognised and the quarries here, west of Burford, provided building material for St Paul's Cathedral and several Oxford colleges.

walk information

➤ **DISTANCE**	6 miles (9.7km)
➤ **MINIMUM TIME**	2hrs 30min
➤ **ASCENT/GRADIENT**	120ft (37m)
➤ **LEVEL OF DIFFICULTY**	
➤ **PATHS**	Fields, tracks and pavement, 11 stiles
➤ **LANDSCAPE**	Streams, fields, open country and villages
➤ **SUGGESTED MAP**	OS Explorer OL45 The Cotswolds
➤ **START/FINISH**	Grid reference: SP 192130
➤ **DOG FRIENDLINESS**	Some care required but can probably be off lead for long stretches without livestock
➤ **PARKING**	Windrush village
➤ **PUBLIC TOILETS**	None on route
➤ **CONTRIBUTOR**	Christopher Knowles

walk directions

1 Walk out of the village, keeping to the left of the church and, after about 100yds (91m), go right, through a gate into a field. Go across this field to the other side, keeping to the left.

2 Go through the right-hand gate and continue across a series of stiles until you emerge in a large field at a wide grass strip (take extra care here, as it is used for 'galloping' horses) with the houses of **Little Barrington** opposite. Cross two thirds of the field, then turn left and head for the hedge at the bottom.

3 Go through a gap to a road. Ahead is the **Fox Inn**. Turn right, enter Little Barrington and turn left along a 'No Through Road' which narrows to a path. Where the path becomes a lane, go left across a bridge and continue, eventually emerging in **Great Barrington** at a cross. Take the road in front of you.

4 Where the wall on your left ends, go left on to a track and immediately right. Stay on this track for a little over 1 mile (1.6km) until you come to a junction of tracks with large hedges before you.

5 Turn left and follow this track until you enter scrubby woodland. Cross the river and follow a grassy track until, just before **Century Wood**, you turn left into a field. Follow the margin of the woods. Cross another bridge into a field and turn half right to the far corner. Go over the bridge, cross a stile and go half left to another stile.

6 Take the track before you and then turn left over another stile. Cross over this field to go through a gate and walk along the right-hand margin on the same line through several fields.

7 Come to a stile at a corner. Go over into the next field and cross it on a right diagonal, in the general direction of a distant village. On the far side go through a gap into another field, with a stone wall on your right. Continue for several fields and pass a **stone barn** to the right, at which point the **River Windrush** will appear to your left. Finally, pass a tin barn to your left-hand side, just as you arrive at a gate by a lane.

8 Opposite, go up to a stile. In the next field follow its perimeter as it goes right and brings you to a stile. Cross to a path and follow it into **Windrush** village.

LEFT: View of the River Windrush near Great Barrington
BELOW: Barrington Park house

Discover the influences of India
through the Cotswold home of
Sir Charles Cockerell.

The Nabob of Sezincote and Bourton-on-the-Hill

For anyone with a fixed idea of the English country house, Sezincote will come as a surprise. It is, as the poet John Betjeman said, 'a good joke, but a good house, too'. Built on the plan of a typical large country house of the era, in every other respect it is thoroughly unconventional. A large copper onion dome crowns the house, whilst at each corner of the roof are finials in the form of miniature minarets. The walls are of Cotswold stone, but the Regency windows, and much of the decoration, owe a lot to Eastern influences.

ABOVE: Bourton-on-the-Hill

Hindu Architecture

Sezincote is a reflection of the fashions of the early 19th century. Just as engravings brought back from Athens had been the inspiration for 18th-century Classicism, so the colourful aqua-tints brought to England from India by returning artists, such as William and Thomas Daniell, were a profound influence on architects and designers. Sezincote was one of the first results of this fashion and the first example of Hindu architecture in England that was actually lived in. Sir Charles Cockerell was a 'nabob', the Hindi-derived word for a European who had made their wealth in the East. On his retirement from the East India Company he had the house built by his brother, Samuel Pepys Cockerell, an architect. The eminent landscape gardener Humphry Repton helped Cockerell to choose the most picturesque elements of Hindu architecture from the Daniells' drawings.

Pavilion Inspiration

Some modern materials, like cast iron, were thought to complement the intricacies of traditional Mogul design. The garden buildings took on elements from Hindu temples, with a lotus shaped temple pool, Hindu columns supporting a bridge and the widespread presence of snakes, sacred bulls and lotus buds. The Prince of Wales was an early visitor. The experience obviously made some impression, as the extremely Mogul Brighton Pavilion arose not long after. Betjeman was a regular guest at Sezincote during his undergraduate days. 'Stately and strange it stood, the nabob's house, Indian without and coolest Greek within, looking from Gloucestershire to Oxfordshire.'

This walks begins and ends in Bourton-on-the-Hill, a pretty village that would be exceptional were it not for traffic streaming through it on the A44. Nevertheless, there is quite a lot to see here. The church owes its impressive features to the fact that the village was formerly owned by Westminster

BELOW: Sezincote House

walk information

➤ **DISTANCE**	3 miles (4.8km)
➤ **MINIMUM TIME**	1hr 15min
➤ **ASCENT/GRADIENT**	85ft (25m) ▲▲▲
➤ **LEVEL OF DIFFICULTY**	🚶🚶🚶
➤ **PATHS**	Tracks, fields and lanes, 7 stiles
➤ **LANDSCAPE**	Hedges, field and spinney on lower part of escarpment
➤ **SUGGESTED MAP**	OS Explorer OL45 The Cotswolds
➤ **START/FINISH**	Grid reference: SP 175324
➤ **DOG FRIENDLINESS**	Under close control – likely to be a lot of livestock
➤ **PARKING**	Street below Bourton-on-the-Hill church, parallel with main road
➤ **PUBLIC TOILETS**	None on route
➤ **CONTRIBUTOR**	Christopher Knowles

Abbey, whose income was handsomely supplemented by sales of wool from their vast flocks on the surrounding hills. There is a fine 15th-century clerestory, lighting an interior notable for its substantial nave columns and a rare bell-metal Winchester Bushel and Peck (8 gallons/35.2 litres and 2 gallons/8.8 litres respectively). These particular standard English measures date from 1816, but their origins go back to the 10th century, when King Edgar (reigned AD 959–975) decreed that standard weights be kept at Winchester and London. They were used to settle disputes, especially when they involved tithes. Winchester measures finally became redundant in 1824 when the Imperial system was introduced, though many Winchester equivalents remain in the United States.

LEFT: Countryside around Bourton-on-the-Hill

walk directions

1 Walk up the road from the **telephone box**, with the church to your right. Turn left down a signposted track between walls. Go through a gate into a field and then continue forward to pass through two more gates.

2 Cross a stile, followed by two kissing gates among the trees. This is the **Sezincote Estate** – go straight ahead, following markers and crossing a drive. Dip down to a gate among trees, with ponds on either side. Go ahead into a field, from where **Sezincote House** is visible to the right.

3 Walk into the next field and go right to the end, aiming for the top, right-hand corner. Pass through a gate to a narrow road and turn left. Walk down this road, passing the **keepers' cottages** to your left, and through a series of gates. The road will bottom out, curve left and right and then bring you to **Upper Rye Farm**. Pass to the right of the farmhouse, go through a gate and, immediately before a barn, turn left along a track and a road.

4 After a second cattle grid, go left over a stile. Follow the edge of the field to a footbridge. Go over it and turn right. Now follow the right-hand margin of the field to a stile in the far corner. Cross this to follow a path through some woodland until you come to a stile and a field and continue on the same line to another stile.

5 Cross a track to another stile and walk on. After a few paces, with Bourton-on-the-Hill plainly visible before you, turn right and follow the path to the next corner. Turn left and pass through three gates. After the third one, walk on for a few paces and turn right through a gate to return to the start.

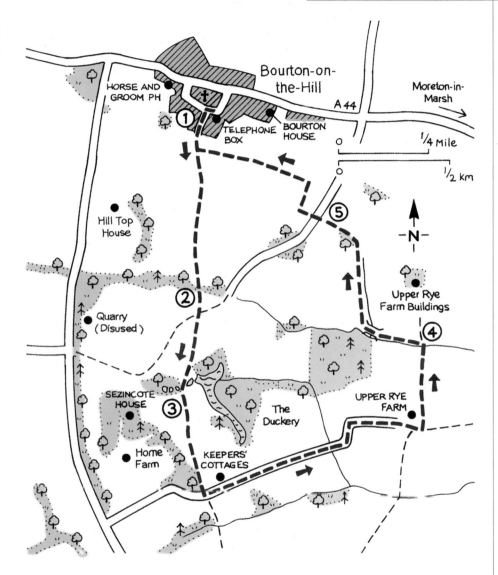

From the Queen of the Cotswolds through the Washpool Valley.

ABOVE: Painswick village
LEFT: Painswick Beacon in Painswick Valley

Painswick's Traditions

Local traditions continue to thrive in Painswick, the 'Queen of the Cotswolds'. These are centred around its well-known churchyard, where the Victorian poet Sydney Dobell is buried. The churchyard is famously filled, not only with the 'table' tombs of 18th-century clothiers, but also with 99 beautifully manicured yew trees, planted in 1792. The legend goes that only 99 will ever grow at any one time, as Old Nick will always kill off the hundredth. Should you be minded to do so, try to count them. You will almost certainly be thwarted, as many of them have grown together, creating arches and hedges.

This old tale has become confused with an ancient ceremony that still takes place here on the Sunday nearest to the Feast of the Nativity of St Mary, in mid-September. This is the 'clipping' ceremony, which has nothing to do with cutting bushes or flowers. It derives from the old Saxon word, 'clyping', which means 'embrace' and is used in conjunction with the church. Traditionally, the children of the village gather together on the Sunday afternoon and join hands to form a circle around the church or churchyard, and advance and retreat to and from the church, singing the Clipping Hymn. Perhaps this ceremony is the distant descendant of an a pagan ceremony involving a ritual dance around an altar bearing a sacrificed animal. The children wear flowers in their hair and are rewarded with a coin and a bun for their efforts. There was, and maybe still is, a special cake baked for the day, known as 'puppy dog pie', in which a small china dog was inserted. Was this a reminder of the ancient ritual sacrifice? There are yew trees in other gardens in the village, many older than those in the churchyard, and one of which is said to have been planted by Elizabeth I.

The other famous tradition that continues to be observed in the area takes place further along the escarpment, at Cooper's Hill. Here, on Spring Bank Holiday Monday, the cheese-rolling races take place. From a spot marked by a maypole, competitors hurtle down an absurdly steep slope in pursuit of wooden discs representing Gloucester cheeses. The winner, or survivor, is presented with a real cheese; but the injury rate is high and there has been a lot of controversy about whether the event should be allowed to continue. Fortunately, tradition has won the day so far and people are still able to break their necks in the pursuit of cheese if they want to.

RIGHT: *Painswick village*

walk information

➤ **DISTANCE**	7½ miles (12.1km)
➤ **MINIMUM TIME**	3hrs 30min
➤ **ASCENT/GRADIENT**	705ft (215m) ▲▲▲
➤ **LEVEL OF DIFFICULTY**	♦♦♦♦
➤ **PATHS**	Fields, tracks, golf course and a green lane, 16 stiles
➤ **LANDSCAPE**	Hills, valleys, villages, isolated farmhouses, extensive views
➤ **SUGGESTED MAP**	OS Explorer 179 Gloucester, Cheltenham & Stroud
➤ **START/FINISH**	Grid reference: SO 865094
➤ **DOG FRIENDLINESS**	Off leads along lengthy stretches, many stiles
➤ **PARKING**	Car park (small fee) near library, just off main road
➤ **PUBLIC TOILETS**	At car park
➤ **CONTRIBUTOR**	Christopher Knowles

walk directions

1 Turn right out of the car park and along the main street. Turn left along the **Gloucester road**, join another road and turn right towards the golf club. Bear left through the car park, turn left along a track and immediately right across a fairway (look out for flying golf balls).

2 Keep to the left of a **cemetery**, then cross another fairway to a woodland path. Continue to a road. After a few paces turn right. Walk along the edge of the golf course to the top of a promontory, passing to the left of a **trig point**. Descend the other side and turn left down a path. At a track go left to a road.

A stroll through the countryside around Slad, backcloth to Laurie Lee's most popular novel.

Walking with Rosie in the Slad Valley

The Slad Valley is one of the least spoiled parts of the Cotswolds, notwithstanding its invariable association with the area's most important literary figure, the poet Laurie Lee (1914–97). And yet he is not instantly remembered for his poetry but for 'Cider With Rosie' (1959). This autobiographical account of his childhood in the Cotswolds has, for thousands of students, been part of their English Literature syllabus.

ABOVE: Cotswolds dry-stone wall
RIGHT: The River Coln through Cassey Compton

walk directions

1 Walk up the lane, signposted 'Crawley'. At the end of the village cross a stile, right, and take the footpath diagonally left across the field, also signposted 'Crawley'. Look right for a view of the ruins of **Minster Lovell Hall** and the circular dovecote. Cross a stile and continue ahead along the path, with a stone wall to your left. The mill chimney ahead on the horizon belongs to Crawley Mill (tastefully restored and now part of a discreet conference centre).

2 Cross a stile and go ahead up a slight incline. Cross another stile, go through a gate and continue on the path, walking up a green tunnel of a lane. Pass above **Crawley Mill**. At the road, turn right and follow this down into **Crawley**. At the bottom, look left to admire the diminutive village green with its stone cross. The **Lamb Inn** is on the left.

3 Turn right and follow the pavement past **Manor Farm**, with its huge pond. Cross the humpback bridge over the **Windrush** – look right for a good view of the old mill house. At the other side of the bridge, cross the road and turn left through a gate, signed 'Witney'. Follow the bridleway beside the stream, marked by a line of willows.

4 At the junction of paths by a gate, look ahead and left to see **New Mill**. Turn right through the gate and walk up the field edge. Pass a gate and cross the road. Climb the stile, go straight on to a second stile, and follow the path down through the woods.

5 At the bottom, cross a stile and follow the path along the fence. The wildflower meadows of **Maggots Grove** lie to your right. Continue over three more stiles and bear left beside the trees. Cross a stile by a meander of the river.

6 Cross a further stile and enter the woods. At a gate bear right, following the arrows, and cross two footbridges. After a short distance cross a bridge over the river. Go through a

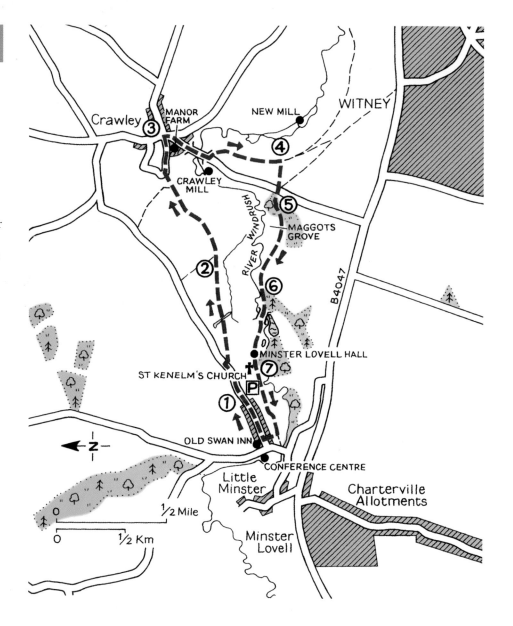

➤ **DISTANCE**	4 miles (6.4km)
➤ **MINIMUM TIME**	1hr 30min
➤ **ASCENT/GRADIENT**	180ft (55m) ▲▲▲
➤ **LEVEL OF DIFFICULTY**	🚶🚶🚶
➤ **PATHS**	Meadows, tracks, pavement and lane, woodland, 17 stiles
➤ **LANDSCAPE**	Shallow, fertile valley of River Windrush
➤ **SUGGESTED MAP**	OS Explorer 180 Oxford, Witney & Woodstock
➤ **START/FINISH**	Grid reference: SP 321114
➤ **DOG FRIENDLINESS**	Lead essential on road through Crawley and Minster Lovell
➤ **PARKING**	Car park (free) at eastern end of Minster Lovell, above church and hall
➤ **PUBLIC TOILETS**	None on route
➤ **CONTRIBUTOR**	Ann F Stonehouse

squeeze gate towards **Minster Lovell Hall**. Climb the stile and go through a gate to explore the ruins.

7 Leave by the top entrance and walk through the churchyard. Cross a slab stile and continue along a grassy path with the village up to your right. Cross a footbridge and stile, and veer to the right. Cross one stile and then another into **Wash Meadow** recreation ground. Keep right and go through a gate on to the high street, with the **Old Swan** pub to your left. Turn right and walk up through the village to the car park.

RIGHT: Old Post House, Minster Lovell

A haunt of the Arts and Crafts pioneer towers above this Worcestershire village.

William Morris's Broadway

If Caspar Wistar were alive today, a springtime visit to Broadway would give him much pleasure. Visitors come in swarms to this Worcestershire village which lies against the edge of the Cotswolds. They buzz around a linear honeycomb, the honey-stone buildings stretching for the best part of a mile (1.6km). Horse chestnut trees flame with pinky-red candelabras and walls drip with the brilliant lilac flowers of wisteria. Caspar, the 18th-century American anatomist after whom the wisteria genus was named, would surely not miss this photo opportunity.

ABOVE: *Broadway village*
RIGHT: *Blue flax field, outside Broadway*

There are many buildings of note in Broadway, not least the partly 14th-century Lygon (pronounced 'Liggon') Arms. The Savoy Group bought the property for £4.7 million in 1986. History has contributed to this price – in 1651, Oliver Cromwell stayed there on the night before the decisive clash in the Civil War, the Battle of Worcester.

Arts and Crafts

Less historic but more affordable is Broadway Tower. The 6th Earl of Coventry's four-storey folly (1799) has served as home to a printing press and a farmhouse, but is best known as a country retreat for William Morris (1834–96). Appropriately, in 1877 he founded the Society for the Protection of Ancient Buildings. Artistically, Morris empathised with the Pre-Raphaelite Brotherhood, a group, primarily of painters, founded in 1849 by William Holman Hunt. They believed that British art had taken a 'wrong turn' under the influence of Raphael, who, with Michelangelo and Leonardo da Vinci had made up the trio of most famous Renaissance artists. Raphael (1483–1520) was catapulted to fame and fortune in his late-twenties when commissioned to paint the stanze (Papal apartments) for Pope Julius II. The English Pre-Raphaelites challenged the teachings of the establishment, producing vividly coloured paintings, lit unconventionally, which had an almost flat appearance.

In 1859, the middle-class Morris married Jane, an 18-year-old, working-class model for Dante Gabriel Rossetti, his British-born mentor. Rossetti's wife committed suicide after two years of their marriage. Rossetti then proceeded to have an affair with Jane. Morris and some friends (including Rossetti!) set up a company producing crafted textile and stained-glass products. Morris was fascinated by pre-industrial techniques. Ironically, only the wealthy could afford to enjoy his essentially medieval art. Disillusioned by the Industrial Revolution, he was attracted to Socialism in the 1870s. He joined the Social Democratic Federation and became increasingly militant. He wrote extensively on Socialism and gave lectures, even on street corners. All the while, he was writing prose and poetry and, when Tennyson died in 1892, Morris was invited to succeed him as poet laureate. He declined the invitation and died four years later.

RIGHT: Cassey Compton

walk directions

1 Walk back down **Church Close** then turn left. At the far end of the church wall turn left, soon passing a tiny, narrow orchard. At a gate before a strip of grass, turn immediately right, to reach a simple log bridge over a rivulet. Turn half left, across uneven pasture. Go to the right-hand field corner. In 40yds (37m) reach a bridge of two railway sleepers beside a stone barn.

2 Cross this to a waymarker through a boggy patch to two stiles. Maintain your line to reach a gate. Cross a large field, now scarcely gaining any height. On joining a vague, sunken lane bear right, to descend briefly to a gate (there's a water trough near by). A tree-lined, dirt track soon reaches another gate within 60yds (55m).

3 Slant uphill, passing in front of a stone building with, sadly, modern windows – Dor Knap (close by) is better. At the woodland ahead turn left. Join a tarmac road, steadily uphill. At the brow turn left, into **Broadway Tower Country Park**, and pass the **Rookery Barn Restaurant**. A tall kissing gate gives access to **Broadway Tower**.

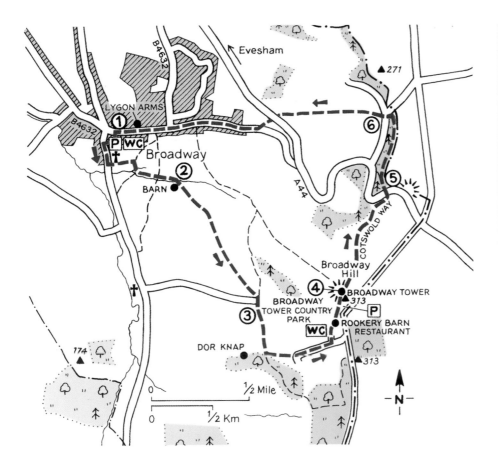

Evesham

B4632

▲271

LYGON ARMS

① P WC Broadway

② BARN

A44

⑥

⑤

COTSWOLD WAY

Broadway Hill

BROADWAY TOWER COUNTRY PARK

③

④ ▲313 BROADWAY TOWER

P

WC ROOKERY BARN RESTAURANT

DOR KNAP

▲313

174 ▲

0 ½ Mile

0 ½ Km

—N—

walk information

➤ **DISTANCE**	5 miles (8km)
➤ **MINIMUM TIME**	2hrs 30min
➤ **ASCENT/GRADIENT**	755ft (230m) ▲▲▲
➤ **LEVEL OF DIFFICULTY**	🚶🚶🚶
➤ **PATHS**	Pasture, rough, tree-root path, pavements, 8 stiles
➤ **LANDSCAPE**	Flat vale rising to escarpment
➤ **SUGGESTED MAP**	OS Explorer OL45 The Cotswolds
➤ **START/FINISH**	Grid reference: SP 094374
➤ **DOG FRIENDLINESS**	Sheep-grazing country (some cattle and horses too) so only off lead in empty fields; some stiles may be tricky
➤ **PARKING**	Pay-and-display, short stay, 4hrs maximum in Church Close, Broadway; longer stay options well-signposted
➤ **PUBLIC TOILETS**	At Church Close car park and at country park
➤ **CONTRIBUTOR**	Nicholas Reynolds

4 Beyond the tower go through a similar gate, then take the little gate immediately on the right. Move down, left, 20yds (18m) to walk in a hollow, through pasture and scrubby hawthorns, to a gate in a dry-stone wall. Soon cross a tractor track and walk parallel to it in a similar hollow, guided by **Cotswold Way** acorn waymarkers. Aim for some bright metal gates amongst trees. Beyond these go straight ahead and in 45yds (41m), at the next marker, bear right, walking above the road. Soon cross it carefully, to footpath signs opposite.

5 Leave the Cotswold Way here. More care is needed in following these next instructions: descend, initially using wooden steps. Ignore a path on the left after 50yds (46m), then after another 50yds (46m) take the yellow arrow waymarker pointing up to the right, over more steps. About 25 paces beyond these step, use a wooden handrail to go down a few more steps. After another 50yds (46m) you'll see an orange **Badger Trail** disc. Go forward on this for just 10yds (9m). Here the orange disc points left, but take the yellow marker, straight ahead. Follow this narrow path (beware many exposed tree roots) near the top of this dense wood. Eventually take steps on the left, down to cross a road junction.

6 Take the field path signposted 'Broadway'. Descend sweetly through pastures. Swing left then right to pass under the new road, emerging near the top end of the old one. Turn right, on to the dead end of **Broadway**'s main street. In the centre, 50yds (46m) beyond three red telephone boxes, turn left, through an arcade, to **Church Close** car park.

A gentle ramble in quintessential Gloucestershire countryside, from a typical village with an atypical place name and atypical ownership.

Guiting Power to the People

It is remarkable how much detailed history is available about English villages, even ones, like Guiting Power, that are distinguished only by their comeliness. Looking from the village green, surrounded by stone cottages, with its church and secluded manor house, it is easy to imagine that very little has changed here in 1,000 years. The eccentric name comes from the Saxon word 'gyte-ing', or torrent, and indeed the name was given not only to Guiting Power but also to neighbouring Temple Guiting, which in the 12th century was owned by the Knights Templars. Guiting Power though, was named after the pre-eminent local family of the 13th century, the Le Poers.

ABOVE: *St Michael's Church, Guiting Power*
RIGHT: *Above Naunton*

What's in a Name?

Over the years the village was variously known as Gything, Getinge, Gettinges Poer, Guyting Poher, Nether Guiting and Lower Guiting. Its current name and spelling date only from 1937. In 1086, *The Domesday Book* noted that there were 'four villagers, three Frenchmen, two riding men, and a priest with two small-holders'. Just under 100 years later the first recorded English fulling mill was in operation at the nearby hamlet of Barton. In 1330 permission was given for a weekly market to be held at Guiting Power, which may explain the current arrangement of the houses about the green. Guiting had its share of the prosperity derived from the 15th-century wool trade, as the church's tower testifies.

Slow to Catch Up

And yet, in other ways, history was slow to catch up with villages like Guiting. Its farmland, for example, was enclosed only in 1798, allowing small landowners, who owned strips of land scattered throughout the parish, to finally consolidate their possessions. Local rights of way were enshrined in law at this time. By the end of the 19th century, the rural depression had reduced the population to 431, and it continued to decline throughout the 20th century. Nonetheless, it is recorded that apart from at least four public houses, there were two grocers, two bakers, two tailors, two carpenters, two policemen and a blacksmith.

There are still two pubs in Guiting Power but everything else, apart from the post office and a grocery store, has disappeared. The village is unusual in that it hasn't succumbed to the inflationary effects of second homeowners pushing up house prices. Much of this is due to Moya Davidson, a resident in the 1930s, who purchased cottages to be rented out locally. Today these are managed by the Guiting Manor Amenity Trust. It has meant that younger people are able to stay in the village and there are still a few families here who can trace their roots back in Guiting Power for several generations.

walk information

➤ **DISTANCE**	5 miles (8km)
➤ **MINIMUM TIME**	2hrs
➤ **ASCENT/GRADIENT**	295ft (90m) ▲▲▲
➤ **LEVEL OF DIFFICULTY**	▲▲▲
➤ **PATHS**	Fields, tracks and country lanes, 10 stiles
➤ **LANDSCAPE**	Woodland, hills and village
➤ **SUGGESTED MAP**	OS Explorer OL45 The Cotswolds
➤ **START /FINISH**	Grid reference: SP 094245
➤ **DOG FRIENDLINESS**	Fairly clear of livestock but many horses on roads
➤ **PARKING**	Car park outside village hall (small fee)
➤ **PUBLIC TOILETS**	None on route
➤ **CONTRIBUTOR**	Christopher Knowles

walk directions

1 From the **village hall** car park, walk down the road to the **village green**. Cross the road to walk down a lane. At the bottom go over a stile into a field and turn right. Walk up the bank, up to another stile. Don't cross the one in front of you but clamber over the one to your right into a field.

2 Turn left and walk straight across this field to another stile. Cross this and two more to pass a farmhouse in **Barton** village. Follow the lane down to a larger road and turn right. Cross a bridge and turn left up a track and, after 100yds (91m), turn right up another track.

3 After a few paces bear left and walk along this track for about a mile (1.6km), until you reach another road. Turn right, walk along here for about 250yds (229m) and turn left on to a track.

4 Follow this all the way to a road, passing a **quarry** as you go. Cross the road and enter a lane descending past a house. This quiet lane will bring you all the way into the village of **Naunton**.

5 At the junction turn right. Walk through the village and cross the pretty stone bridge by the old mill, passing the old **rectory** to the left and the church concealed to the right. (To get to the **Black Horse Inn**, turn left and walk along the street for 400yds (366m). Return by entering a drive opposite the pub, turning sharp right over a stile, and walking back along the side of the river to emerge at a road near the church, where you turn left.) Continue up, out of the village.

6 After ¼ mile (400m), turn right over a stile into a field. Turn left, walk to a stile and go into the next field. Cross this field, enter the next one and follow the path to the right of some trees to a gate at the road.

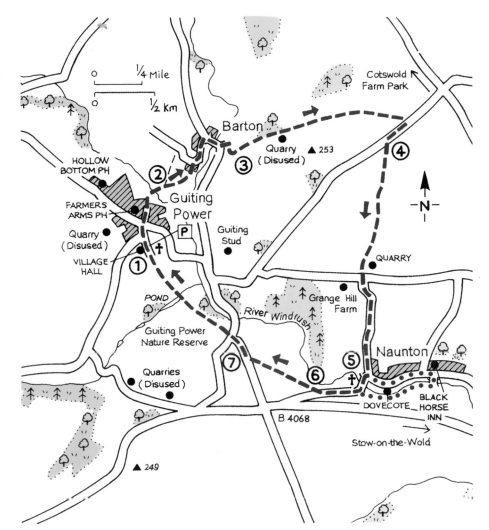

7 Turn right and continue to a junction at the end. Cross over to enter a field and walk straight across. At the end go down steps and pass to the right of a pond. Walk across the next field, then cross a stile to walk to the left of the **church**.

LEFT: Dovecote in Naunton

From Chipping Norton to an ancient site associated with a charming legend.

Myths of the Rollright Stones

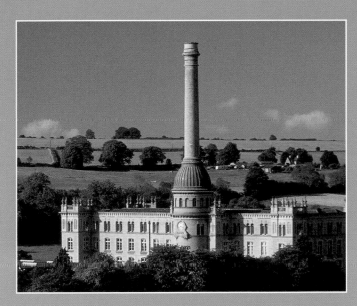

LEFT: The stone circle at Great Rollright
ABOVE: The Bliss Tweed Mill, Chipping Norton

Commanding a splendid position overlooking the hills and valleys of the north east Cotswolds, the Rollright Stones comprise the Whispering Knights, the King's Men and the King Stone. These intriguing stones are steeped in myth. It seems a king was leading his army here while five of his knights stood together conspiring against him. The king met a witch near by, who told him he would be King of England if he could see the settlement of Long Compton in seven long strides. As he approached the top of the ridge, a mound of earth suddenly rose up before him, preventing him from seeing the village and so the king, his soldiers and his knights were turned to stone.

Mystical Theories

In reality, the Rollright Stones form a group of prehistoric megalithic monuments created from large natural boulders found within about 600yds (549m) of the site. The stones are naturally pitted, giving them astonishing and highly unusual shapes. The Whispering Knights, of which there are five, are the remains of a Portal Dolmen burial chamber, probably constructed around 3800–3000 BC, long before the stone circle. The King Stone stands alone and apart from the others, just across the county boundary in Warwickshire. The 8ft-tall (2.4m) standing stone was almost certainly erected to mark the site of a Bronze Age cemetery which was in use around 1800–1500 BC.

Finally, you come to the King's Men Stone Circle – a ceremonial monument thought to have been built around 2500–2000 BC. There are over 70 stones here, but it has been said they are impossible to count! Originally there were about 105 stones forming a continuous wall except for one narrow entrance. The King's Men Stones are arranged in an unditched circle about 100ft (30m) across and ranging in size from just a few inches to 7ft (2m). Here and there the stones are so close they almost touch.

It is not clear what the stone circle was used for but it may well have had some significance in religious and secular ceremonies. Between 200 and 300 people can fit within the circle, though it is not known how many people would attend these ceremonies or what form they took. Most mysterious of all is why this particular site was chosen. Many visitors to the Rollright Stones have questioned their origin over the years but they remain a mystery. Appropriate for such a legend as this, the remote hilltop setting of these timeless stones has more than a hint of the supernatural about it.

RIGHT: Little Rollright

walk directions

1 Follow the **A44** downhill. Pass Penhurst School, then veer right, through a kissing gate. Skirt the left-hand edge of the recreation ground and aim for a gate. Descend to a bridge and, when the path forks, keep right. Go up the slope to reach three stiles and keep ahead along the right-hand edge of the field. Make for gate and drop down to some double gates in the corner.

2 Cross a track just beyond the gates and walk towards Salford, keeping the hedge on the left. Continue into the village and soon turn right by a patch of grass and a sign, 'Trout Lakes – **Rectory Farm**'.

3 Follow the track to a right-hand bend. Go straight ahead here, following the field edge. Make for a gate ahead and turn right in the next field. About 100yds (91m) before the field corner, turn left and follow the path across to an opening in the boundary. Veer left, then immediately right to skirt the field. Cross a little stream and maintain your direction in the next field to reach the road.

4 Turn left, then left again to reach **Little Rollright**. After visiting the church, retrace your steps to the **D'Arcy Dalton Way** on the left. Follow the path up the field slope to the road. Cross over and continue on the way between fields. Head for some trees and approach a stile. Don't cross it; instead, turn left and skirt the field, passing close to the **Whispering Knights**.

5 On reaching the road, turn left and visit the site of the **Rollright Stones**. Return to the Whispering Knights, head down the field to the stile and cross it to an immediate second stile. Walk ahead along a grassy path and turn right at the next stile towards **Brighthill Farm**. Pass alongside the buildings to a stile, head diagonally right down the field to a further stile. Keep the boundary on your right and head

75

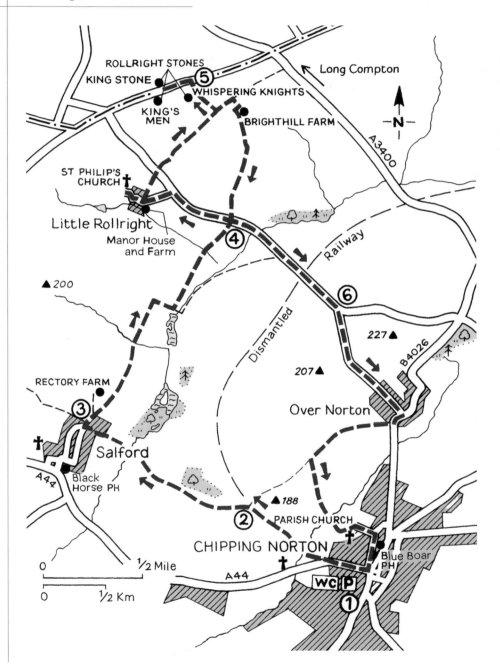

walk information

➤ **DISTANCE**	8 miles (12.9km)
➤ **MINIMUM TIME**	4hrs
➤ **ASCENT/GRADIENT**	295ft (90m) ▲▲▲
➤ **LEVEL OF DIFFICULTY**	🚶🚶🚶
➤ **PATHS**	Field paths and tracks, country roads, 9 stiles
➤ **LANDSCAPE**	Picturesque rolling hills on the Oxfordshire/Warwickshire border
➤ **SUGGESTED MAP**	OS Explorer 191 Banbury, Bicester & Chipping Norton
➤ **START/FINISH**	Grid reference: SP 312270
➤ **DOG FRIENDLINESS**	Under control or on lead across farmland, one lengthy stretch of country road and busy streets in Chipping Norton
➤ **PARKING**	Free car park off A44, in centre of Chipping Norton
➤ **PUBLIC TOILETS**	At car park
➤ **CONTRIBUTOR**	Nick Channer

for a stile in the bottom right corner of the field. Make for the bottom right corner of the next field, go through a gate and skirt the field, turning left at the road.

6 Keep right at the next fork and head towards the village of **Over Norton**. Walk through the village to the T-junction. Turn right and when the road swings to the left by Cleeves Corner, join a track signposted 'Salford'. When the hedges give way, look for a waymark on the left. Follow the path down the slope, make for two kissing gates and then follow the path alongside a stone wall to reach the parish church. Join Church Lane and follow it as far as the T-junction. Turn right and return to the town centre.

The vast bulk of the ancient fort of Uley Bury forms the centrepiece for this walk along the Cotswold escarpment.

Uley and its Magnificent Fort on the Hill

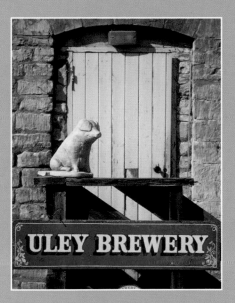

ABOVE: Uley Brewery, renowned for producing distinctive local beers

Uley is a pretty village, strung along a wide street at the foot of a high, steep hill. It is distinctive for several reasons. It has its own brewery, which produces some fine beers, including Uley Bitter and Uley Old Spot. In the past, the village specialised in the production of 'Uley Blue' cloth, which was used in military uniforms. And then there is Uley Bury, dating back to the Iron Age and one of the finest hill forts in the Cotswolds.

Peaceful Settlements

There are many hundreds of Iron-Age forts throughout England and Wales. They are concentrated in Cornwall, south west Wales and the Welsh Marches, with secondary concentrations throughout the Cotswolds, North Wales and Wessex. Although the term 'hill fort' is generally used in connection with these settlements, the term can be misleading. There are many that were built on level ground and there are many that were not used purely for military purposes – often they were simply settlements located on easily defended sites. Broadly speaking, there are five types, classified according to the nature of the site on which they were built, rather than, say, the date of their construction. Contour forts were built more or less along the perimeter edge of a hilltop; promontory forts were built on a spur, surrounded by natural defences on two or more sides; valley and plateau forts (two types) depended heavily on artificial defences and were located, as their names suggest, in valleys or on flat land respectively; and multiple-enclosure forts were usually built in a poor strategic position on the slope of a hill and were perhaps used as stockades.

Natural Defences

Uley Bury, covering about 38 acres (15.4ha), is classified as an inland promontory fort and was built in the 6th century BC. It falls away on three sides; the fourth side, which faces away from the escarpment, is protected by specially constructed ramparts which would have been surmounted by a wooden palisade. The natural defences – that is, the Cotswold escarpment, facing west – were also strengthened by the construction of a wide and deep ditch, as well as two additional ramparts, an inner one and an outer one, between which the footpath largely threads its

course. The three main entrances were at the northern, eastern and southern corners. These, being the most vulnerable parts of the fort, would have been fortified with massive log barriers.

Although some tribespeople would have lived permanently in huts within the fort, most would have lived outside, either on other parts of the hill or in the valleys below. In an emergency, therefore, there was space for those who lived outside the fort to take shelter within. Eventually the fort was taken over by the Dobunni tribe – Celtic interlopers from mainland Europe who arrived about 100 BC – and appears to have been occupied by them throughout the Roman era.

FAR LEFT: Hetty Pegler's Tump
LEFT: The Church of St Giles in Uley

walk information

➤ **DISTANCE**	3 miles (4.8km)
➤ **MINIMUM TIME**	1hr 30min
➤ **ASCENT/GRADIENT**	345ft (105m) ▲▲▲
➤ **LEVEL OF DIFFICULTY**	🚶
➤ **PATHS**	Tracks and fields, 3 stiles
➤ **LANDSCAPE**	Valley, meadows, woodland and open hilltop
➤ **SUGGESTED MAP**	OS Explorer 168 Stroud, Tetbury and Malmesbury
➤ **START/FINISH**	Grid reference: ST 789984
➤ **DOG FRIENDLINESS**	Good – little or no livestock, few stiles
➤ **PARKING**	Main street of Uley
➤ **PUBLIC TOILETS**	None on route
➤ **CONTRIBUTOR**	Christopher Knowles

A picturesque walk around three of Gloucestershire's finest villages.

Stanton and Stanway from Snowshill

Cotswold villages are radiant examples of English vernacular architecture, but they haven't always been the prosperous places they are today. Many, like Stanton and Snowshill, were once owned by the great abbeys. With the dissolution of the monasteries they became the property of private landlords. Subsistence farmers were edged out by the introduction of short leases and enclosure of the open fields. Villagers who had farmed their own strips of land became labourers. The number of small farmers decreased and, with the innovations of the Industrial Revolution, so too did the demand for labour.

ABOVE: Cranham Woods
RIGHT: The Cotswolds Way Path

To the Cities

People left the countryside in droves to work in the industrial towns and cities. Cotswold villages, once at the core of the most important woollen industry in medieval Europe, gradually became impoverished backwaters. However the villages themselves resisted decay. Unlike villages in many other parts of Britain, their buildings were made of stone. Enlightened landlords, who cherished their innate beauty, turned them into huge restoration projects.

Enlightened Landlords

The three villages encountered on this walk are living reminders of this process. Snowshill, together with Stanton, was once owned by Winchcombe Abbey. In 1539 it became the property of Henry VIII's sixth wife, Catherine Parr. The manor house was transformed into the estate's administrative centre and remained in the Parr family until 1919. Then the estate was bought by Charles Wade, a sugar plantation owner. He restored the house and devoted his time to amassing an extraordinary collection of art and artefacts, which he subsequently bequeathed to the National Trust. Now forming the basis of a museum, his collection, from Japanese armour to farm machinery, is of enormous appeal. Next on this walk comes Stanway, a small hamlet at the centre of a large estate owned by Lord Neidpath. The most striking feature here is the magnificent gatehouse to the Jacobean Stanway House, a gem of Cotswold architecture built around 1630.

Restored Houses

The village of Stanton comes last on this walk. It was rescued from decay and oblivion in 1906 by the architect Sir Philip Stott. He bought and restored Stanton Court and many of the village's 16th-century houses. The peaceful parish church is located along a lane leading from the market cross. It has two pulpits (one dating from the 14th century, the other Jacobean) and a west gallery added by the Victorian restorer Sir Ninian Comper. The founder of Methodism, John Wesley, preached here in 1733.

LEFT: Snowshill village

walk directions

1 Walk out of Snowshill village with the **church** on your left. After ¼ mile (400m) turn right, to walk down a lane. After another ¼ mile (400m), at a corner, turn left up to a gate and enter a field.

2 Go quarter left to a gate. In the next field go half right to the far corner and left along a track. Take the second footpath on the right through a gate into a field and walk across to another field. Cross this to a track.

3 Walk down the track. After 275yds (251m), turn right on to a stony track, descending steeply through **Lidcombe Wood**. Where it flattens out, a farm will come into view across fields to the right, after which the track bears left. Continue straight on along a narrow footpath to a road.

4 Walk along the pavement and, after 500yds (457m), turn right over a stile into a small orchard. Walk across this, bearing slightly right, to arrive at a gate. Go through this and walk with a high wall to your right, to reach a road.

5 Turn right and pass the impressive entrance to **Stanway House** and **Stanway church**. Follow the road as it goes right. Shortly after another entrance turn right over a stile. Go half left to another stile and in the next large field go half right.

6 Now walk all the way into **Stanton**, following the regular and clear waymarkers of the **Cotswold Way**. After 1 mile (1.6km) you will arrive at a stile at the edge of Stanton. Turn left along a track to a junction. Turn right here and walk through the village. Where the road goes left, walk straight on, passing the stone cross and then another footpath. Climb up to pass the **Mount Inn**. Behind it walk up a steep, shaded path to a gate. Then walk straight up the hill (ignoring a path to the right after a few paces). Climb all the way to the top to meet a lane.

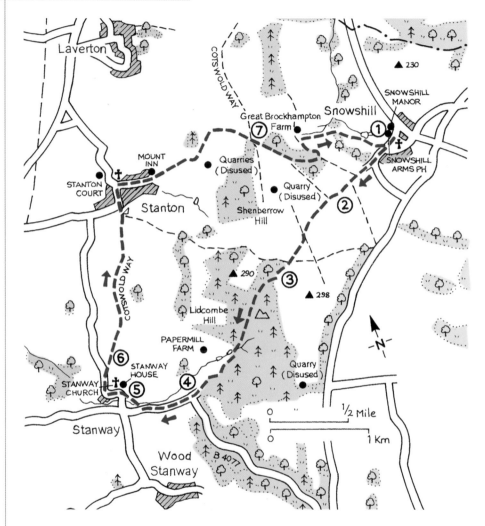

walk information

➤ **DISTANCE**	6¼ miles (10.1km)	
➤ **MINIMUM TIME**	2hrs 45min	
➤ **ASCENT/GRADIENT**	625ft (190m) ▲▲▲	
➤ **LEVEL OF DIFFICULTY**	🚶🚶🚶	
➤ **PATHS**	Tracks, grassland and pavement, 7 stiles	
➤ **LANDSCAPE**	High grassland, open wold, wide-ranging views and villages	
➤ **SUGGESTED MAP**	OS Explorer OL45 The Cotswolds	
➤ **START/FINISH**	Grid reference: SP 096337	
➤ **DOG FRIENDLINESS**	On leads – livestock on most parts of walk	
➤ **PARKING**	Snowshill village	
➤ **PUBLIC TOILETS**	None on route	
➤ **CONTRIBUTOR**	Christopher Knowles	

RIGHT: Fields near Stanton village

7 Walk down the lane for 250yds (229m) then turn left over a stile into woodland. Follow the path, going left at a fork. At the bottom, cross a stile on to a lane and turn left. Walk along here for 200yds (183m). Before a cottage turn right over a stile into a scrubby field. Cross to the far side and turn right through a gate. Continue to a stile on your right, cross it and turn left. Follow the margin of this grassy area to a gate and then follow the path back into **Snowshill**.

A walk that takes you past Kiftsgate Court and Hidcote Manor Garden, two early 20th-century creations of international repute.

Gloucestershire's Gardens around Mickleton

This walk takes you within striking distance of two of the finest planned gardens in the country. The first, Kiftsgate Court, is the lesser known of the two but nonetheless demands a visit. The house itself is primarily Victorian, whilst the garden was created immediately after World War One by Heather Muir, who was a close friend of Major Johnston, the creator of the nearby Hidcote Manor Garden. Kiftsgate's gardens are designed around a steep hillside overlooking Mickleton and the Vale of Evesham, with terraces, paths, flowerbeds and shrubs.

ABOVE AND RIGHT: Hidcote Manor Gardens, owned by the National Trust

Major Johnson's Rooms

The second horticultural treat is Hidcote Manor Garden, part of the little hamlet of Hidcote Bartrim. This garden is the fruit of over 40 years of work by Major Lawrence Johnson, an East Coast American who purchased the 17th-century manor house in 1907 and gave it to the National Trust in 1948. Many people consider it be one of the greatest of English gardens, and certainly it is one of the most influential. Hidcote grew from almost nothing – when Major Johnson first arrived there was a just a cedar tree and a handful of beeches on 11 acres

(4.5ha) of open wold. To some extent it reconciles the formal and informal schools of garden design. Hidcote is not one garden but several. Like Kiftsgate, it is laid out in a series of 'outdoor rooms', as they have been described, with walls of stone and of hornbeam, yew and box hedge. These rooms are themed, having names such as the White Garden and the Fuchsia Garden, for example. There is also a wild garden growing around a stream, as well as lawns and carefully placed garden ornaments that help to create a bridge between the order within and the disorder without.

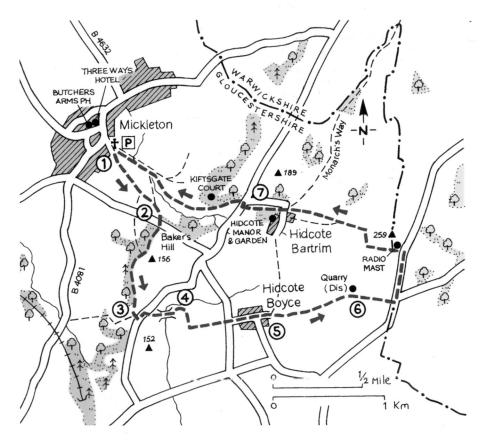

Have a Butchers

This walk begins in Mickleton, at the foot of the Cotswold escarpment, below these two fine gardens. Clearly a Cotswold village, notwithstanding its mixture of stone, thatch and timber, the parish church at the village edge lurks behind a striking house in the so-called Cotswold Queen Anne style. It has a 14th-century tower and an interesting monument to the 18th-century quarry owner from Chipping Campden, Thomas Woodward. Near the hotel in the village centre is a Victorian memorial fountain designed by William Burges, the architect behind Cardiff Castle. There is also a fine butcher's shop here, a sight to behold, especially in autumn, when it's festooned with locally shot pheasant. As if to further enhance the village's Cotswold credentials, this was also the birthplace of Endymion Porter, a patron of the Cotswold Olimpick Games on Dover's Hill.

walk directions

1 With your back to the **church**, turn right up a bank to a gate. Cross a field on a right diagonal to a gate at a thicket. Follow a path through trees. Emerge into a field and follow its left margin to a gate at the end.

2 In the next field, go half right to a gate in the corner. Cross a road and go up some steps to a stile. Turn right to walk around the edge of the field as it bears left. After 250yds (229m), take a path among trees, a steep bank eventually appearing down to the right. The path brings you to a field and then to a barn.

3 At the barn, turn left on to a track. Just about opposite, keep left of a hedge, following the edge of a field to the bottom corner. Go through a gap to a bridge across a stream and turn left.

4 Follow the margin of the field as it goes right and then right again. Continue until you come to a gate on the left. Go through this and walk until you reach another gate at a road. Walk ahead through **Hidcote Boyce**. Where the road goes right, stay ahead to pass through a farmyard.

5 Beyond a gate, take a rising track for just over ¼ mile (400m). Where this track appears to fork, stay to the left to enter a field. Bear left and then right around a hedge and head for a gate. In an area of grassy mounds, stay to the left of a barn and head for a gate visible in the top left corner.

6 Follow the next field edge to a road. Turn sharp left to follow the lesser road. Immediately before a radio transmission mast, turn left on to a track and follow this all the way down to pass to the left of **Hidcote Manor Garden**. After passing the garden's main entrance, go left through a gate into shrubland and turn right. Follow the path to a field and cross it to a gate on the far side.

walk information

➤ **DISTANCE**	5½ miles (8.8km)
➤ **MINIMUM TIME**	2hrs 30min
➤ **ASCENT/GRADIENT**	625ft (190m) ▲▲▲
➤ **LEVEL OF DIFFICULTY**	👥👥👥
➤ **PATHS**	Fields, firm tracks, some possibly muddy woodland, 12 stiles
➤ **LANDSCAPE**	Woodland, open hills and villages
➤ **SUGGESTED MAP**	OS Explorer 205 Stratford-upon-Avon & Evesham
➤ **START/FINISH**	Grid reference: SP 162434
➤ **DOG FRIENDLINESS**	On leads in livestock fields, good open stretches elsewhere
➤ **PARKING**	Free car park at church
➤ **PUBLIC TOILETS**	None on route
➤ **CONTRIBUTOR**	Christopher Knowles

7 At the road turn right and then, before **Kiftsgate Court**, turn left through a gate and descend through a field. Pass through some trees and follow the left-hand side of the next field until you come to a gate on the left. Go through this and cross to another gate. Follow the edge of the next field. Where the field opens up head just to the left of **Mickleton church**. Go through a gate leading between the two cemeteries to return to the start.

PAGE 90 AND RIGHT: Hidcote Manor Gardens

Combine a stroll around England's finest medieval village with a riverside walk and a visit to Lacock Abbey, home of photographic pioneer Fox Talbot.

Lacock – the Birthplace of Photography

ABOVE: *Sign of the Angel Hotel, Lacock*

Timeless Lacock could stand as the pattern of the perfect English village, with its twisting streets, packed with attractive buildings from the 15th to 18th centuries, possessing all the character and atmosphere of medieval England. Half-timbering, lichen grey stone, red-brick and whitewashed façades crowd together and above eye-level, uneven upper storeys, gabled ends and stone roofs blend with charming ease. With so much to enjoy, plan to spend the whole day exploring the village and abbey.

Fox Talbot and Lacock Abbey

Entirely owned and preserved by the National Trust since 1944, Lacock is amongst England's most beautiful villages.

Of all the outstanding buildings in the village, Lacock Abbey, on the outskirts, is the most beautiful. It began as an Augustinian nunnery in 1232, but after the Reformation Sir William Sharrington used the remains to build a Tudor mansion, preserving the fine cloister court, sacristy and chapter house, and adding a romantic octagonal tower, a large courtyard and twisting chimney stacks.

The abbey passed to the Talbot family through marriage and they Gothicised the south elevation and added the oriel windows. Surrounded by peaceful water-meadows bordering the River Avon, this was the setting for the experiments of William Henry Fox Talbot (1800–77), which in 1835 led to the creation of the world's first photographic negative. You can see some of Fox Talbot's work and equipment, alongside interesting photographic exhibitions, in the beautifully restored 16th-century barn at the gates to the abbey.

Village Highlights

Architectural gems to note as you wander around Lacock's ancient streets include the timber-framed Sign of the Angel Inn, on Church Street, which retains its medieval layout, a 16th-century doorway and the passage through which horses would pass. Near by, Cruck House, with one of its cruck beams exposed, is a rare example of this 14th-century building method. Further along, you'll pass King John's Hunting Lodge, reputed to be even older than the abbey, and St Cyriac's Church, which contains the grandiose Renaissance tomb of Sir William Sharrington. In West Street, the George Inn dates back to 1361 and features a huge open fire with a dogwheel, which was connected to the spit on the fire and turned by a dog called a Turnspit. Next to the pub, take a look at the bus shelter; it was formerly the smithy.

ABOVE: Lacock Abbey
RIGHT: Cloisters at Lacock Abbey

On the corner of East Street is the magnificent 14th-century tithe barn with fine curved timbers. This was once used to store the rents which were paid to the abbey in kind, such as corn, hides and fleeces. The building later became the market hall as Lacock flourished into a thriving wool trading centre. Finally, don't miss the 18th-century domed lock-up next door. This is known as a 'blind house', since many of its overnight prisoners were drunks. You may recognise Lacock's medieval streets as the backdrop to several television costume dramas, notably Jane Austen's *Pride and Prejudice* (1995) and *Emma* (1996), and Daniel Defoe's rather bawdy *Moll Flanders* (1996).

walk directions

1 From the car park, cross the road and follow the path into **Lacock**. Turn right into **East Street** opposite the **Red Lion** and walk down to **Church Street**. Turn left, then keep left into **West Street** and go left again into **High Street**.

2 Walk back down **East Street**. Turn right along **Church Street** and bear left in front of the church to cross a bridge over the **Bide Brook**. Follow the path by the stream then up the lane to the end of the road.

3 Go through the kissing gate on your right and follow the tarmac path across the field to a gate. Pass cottages to a lane, turn right, and then right again to cross the **River Avon**. Climb the stile on your left. Bear diagonally right across the field to a stile and cross the lane and stile opposite. Follow the path to two squeeze stiles and turn left around the field edge.

4 Climb the stile on your left and turn right along the field edge. Follow the path through scrub to a stile and proceed ahead beside the old **Wilts and Berks Canal**. Pass an old bridge, climb a stile into woodland and turn immediately right along a narrow path to a stile. Turn left along the field edge, keep ahead across the next field to a stile and head uphill to a stile.

5 Proceed ahead to a gate and cross the next field to a gate. Join a track, cross a metalled farm drive and continue to a gate. Ascend a grassy track to a gate and walk uphill towards a house. Before a gate, turn right across the top of the field to reach double stiles. Bear half right to a gate and ascend the farm drive through woodland, then uphill to a gate. Continue to a lane.

6 Turn left, then cross the stile on the right before a house. Keep to the left-hand field edge, cross a stile and bear

On the Thames Path to the home of

William Morris.

Buscot to Kelmscott

The village of Kelmscott is famous for its connections with the founder of the Arts and Crafts Movement, William Morris (1834–96). Today he is best remembered for his furnishing and decorative designs, rich with flowers, leaves and birds, still popular on fabric and wallpaper.

RIGHT: Stonecarving of William Morris, Kelmscott
FAR RIGHT: Canal boat on the River Thames, Lechlade
PAGE 100: Kelmscott Manor

Take a walk on the wilder side of Bourton-on-the-Water to see its natural regeneration.

Regenerating Bourton-on-the-Water

LEFT AND ABOVE: Around the village in Bourton-on-the Water

Despite the popularity of Bourton-on-the-Water, the crowds are easily left behind by walking briefly eastwards to a chain of redundant gravel pits. In the 1970s these were landscaped and filled with water and fish. As is the way of these things, for some time the resulting lakes looked every inch the artificial creations they were, but now they have bedded into their surroundings and seem to be an integral part of the landscape.

walk information

➤ **DISTANCE**	4¾ miles (7.7km)
➤ **MINIMUM TIME**	2hrs
➤ **ASCENT/GRADIENT**	230ft (70m) ▲▲▲
➤ **LEVEL OF DIFFICULTY**	🚶🚶🚶
➤ **PATHS**	Track and field, can be muddy and wet in places, 26 stiles
➤ **LANDSCAPE**	Sweeping valley views, lakes, streams, hills and village
➤ **SUGGESTED MAP**	OS Explorer OL45 The Cotswolds
➤ **START/FINISH**	Grid reference: SP 169208
➤ **DOG FRIENDLINESS**	Some stiles may be awkward for dogs; occasional livestock
➤ **PARKING**	Pay-and-display car park on Station Road
➤ **PUBLIC TOILETS**	At car park
➤ **CONTRIBUTOR**	Christopher Knowles

BELOW: *Local delicacies in Bourton-on -the-Water*

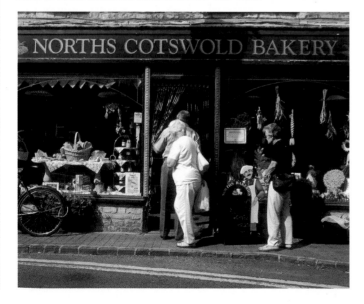

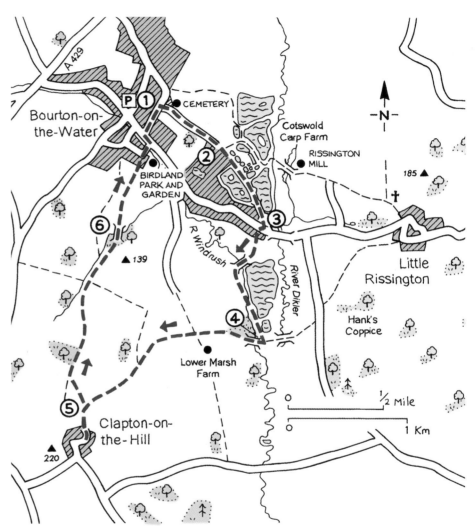

Extending the Walk

You can extend this walk to include the pretty village of **Little Rissington.** As you leave Bourton on the lane after the **cemetery**, at Point ②, follow a path to the left, past lakes and meadows to **Rissington Mill**. Field paths take you into the village and you can meet up with the main route again across the bridge near Point ④.

Explore this architectural treasure of a
town and the adjacent Corsham Park.

Corsham – a Wealthy Weaving Town

Warm, cream-coloured Bath stone characterises this handsome market town, situated on the southern edge of the Cotswolds. An air of prosperity pervades the streets, where the baroque-pedimented 17th-century Hungerford Almshouses mix with 15th-century Flemish gabled cottages and larger Georgian residences. Architectural historian Nikolaus Pevsner wrote: 'Corsham has no match in Wiltshire for the wealth of good houses.'

LEFT: Archway to Corsham Court

the family's collection of 16th- and 17th-century Italian and Flemish Master paintings and statuary. The house and park you see today are principally the work of 'Capability' Brown, John Nash and Thomas Bellamy. Brown built the gabled wings that house the state rooms and magnificent 72-ft (22-m) long picture gallery, and laid out the park, including the avenues, Gothic bathhouse and the 13-acre (5-ha) lake.

Round off your walk with a tour of the house. This includes, an outstanding collection of more than 140 paintings, including pictures by Rubens, Turner, Reynolds and Van Dyck, fine statuary and bronzes, and the famous collection of English furniture, notably pieces by Robert Adam and Thomas Chippendale.

You may also recognise the house as the backdrop for the film *The Remains of the Day* (1993) starring Anthony Hopkins.

RIGHT: A charming Cotswold Cottage

walk directions

1 Turn left out of the car park, then left again along **Post Office Lane** to reach the **High Street**. Turn left, pass the tourist information centre and turn right into Church Street. Pass the impressive entrance to **Corsham Court** and enter **St Bartholomew's churchyard**.

2 Follow the path left to a gate and walk ahead to join the main path across **Corsham Park**. Turn left and walk along the south side of the park, passing **Corsham Lake**, to reach a stile and gate. Keep straight on along a fenced path beside a track to a kissing gate and cross a field to a stile and lane.

3 Turn left, pass **Park Farm**, a splendid stone farmhouse on your left, and shortly take the waymarked footpath, right, along a drive to pass **Rose and Unicorn House**. Cross a stile and follow the right-hand field edge to a stile, then bear half-left to a stone stile in the field corner. Ignore the path arrowed right and head straight across the field to a further stile and lane.

4 Take the footpath opposite, bearing half-left to a stone stile to the left of a cottage. Maintain direction and pass through a field entrance to follow the path along the left-hand side of a field to a stile in the corner. Turn left along the road for ½ mile (800m) to the **A4**.

5 Go through the gate in the wall on your left and follow the worn path right, across the centre of parkland pasture to a metal kissing gate. Proceed ahead to reach a kissing gate on the edge of woodland. Follow the wide path to a further gate and bear half-right to a stile.

6 Keep ahead on a worn path across the field and along the field edge to a gate. Continue to a further gate with fine views right to **Corsham Court**. Follow the path right along the field edge, then where it curves right, bear left to join the path beside the churchyard wall to a stile.

7 Turn left down the avenue of trees to a gate and the town centre, noting the lovely stone almshouses on your left. Turn right to walk along **Pickwick Road** and then right again along the pedestrianised **High Street**. Turn left back along **Post Office Lane** to the car park.

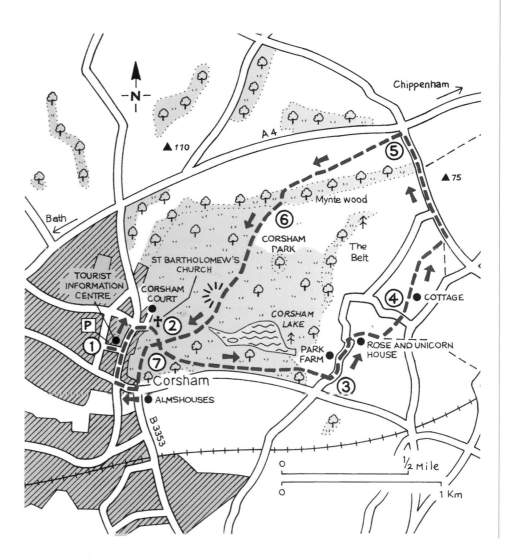

1	21	41	61	81	101	121	141	161	181
2	22	42	62	82	102	122	142	162	182
3	23	43	63	83	103	123	143	163	183
4	(24)	44	64	84	104	124	144	164	184
5	25	45	65	85	105	125	145	165	185
6	26	46	66	86	106	126	146	166	186
7	27	47	67	87	107	127	147	167	187
8	28	48	68	88	108	128	148	168	188
9	29	49	69	89	109	129	149	169	189
10	30	50	70	90	110	130	150	170	190
11	31	51	71	91	111	131	151	171	191
12	32	52	72	92	112	132	152	172	192
13	33	53	73	93	113	133	153	173	193
14	34	54	74	94	114	134	154	174	194
15	35	55	75	95	115	135	155	175	195
16	36	56	76	96	116	136	156	176	196
17	37	57	77	97	117	137	157	177	197
18	38	58	78	98	118	138	158	178	198
19	39	59	79	99	119	139	159	179	199
20	40	60	80	100	120	140	160	180	200

201	216	231	246	261	276	291	306	321	336
202	217	232	247	262	277	292	307	322	337
203	218	233	248	263	278	293	308	323	338
204	219	234	249	264	279	294	309	324	339
205	220	235	250	265	280	295	310	325	340
206	221	236	251	266	281	296	311	326	341
207	222	237	252	267	282	297	312	327	342
208	223	238	253	268	283	298	313	328	343
209	224	239	254	269	284	299	314	329	344
210	225	240	255	270	285	300	315	330	345
211	226	241	256	271	286	301	316	331	346
212	227	242	257	272	287	302	317	332	347
213	228	243	258	273	288	303	318	333	348
214	229	244	259	274	289	304	319	334	349
215	230	245	260	275	290	305	320	335	350